The Creacion of the World

Garland Medieval Texts

Number 3

Garland Medieval Texts

A.S.G. Edwards
General Editor

Number 1:
The Commonplace Book of Robert Reynes of Acle:
An Edition of Tanner MS 407
Edited by Cameron Louis

Number 2:
The Isle of Ladies
or The Ile of Pleasaunce
Edited by Anthony Jenkins

Number 3:
The Creacion of the World:
A Critical Edition and Translation
Edited and Translated by Paula Neuss

Number 4:
Scotish Feilde and Flodden Feilde:
Two Flodden Poems
Edited by Ian F. Baird

The Creacion of the World
A Critical Edition and Translation

edited and translated by
Paula Neuss

GARLAND PUBLISHING, INC.
NEW YORK & LONDON
1983

Library of Congress Cataloging in Publication Data

Main entry under title:
The Creacion of the world.

(Garland medieval texts ; no. 3)
Cornish and English.
According to colophon of original manuscript, written by William Jordan; he is believed to have been the scribe and not the author—cf. Introd.
Translation of: Gwreans an bys.
Bibliography: p.
1. Mysteries and miracle-plays, Cornish. 2. Cornish drama. I. Neuss, Paula. II. Jordan, William, fl. 1611. III. Title. IV. Series.
PB2591.G8E5 1983 891.6'72 81–23528
ISBN 0–8240–9447–6

Printed on acid-free, 250-year-life paper
Manufactured in the United States of America

To
Ronald and Peggy Neuss

Contents

1. *God the Father creates the World*, Codex, 2554, Osterreichische National Bibliotek, f4.

Preface

The Creacion of the World, a Cornish miracle play with stage directions in English, is of great interest to students of mediaeval drama and the mediaeval theatre, for whom this book is primarily intended. There is also a complete cycle in Cornish extant, the *Ordinalia*, which contains three plays to be shown on three consecutive days, and a Cornish saint's play, *Bewnans Meriasek*. These five plays (and a Passion poem of 1036 lines) are our only example of original literature written in the Cornish language, apart from a few short poems and fragments. The plays have naturally been studied by those interested in Cornish philology but have tended to be neglected by students of the early drama because of the difficulties involved in reading the text. Translations of all the plays were made in the nineteenth century, but they have long been out of print. Because the translators were working on material hitherto almost untouched, these versions also contain a number of errors. Extracts from the plays in modern Unified Cornish have been produced in mimeograph by the Federation of Old Cornwall Societies, but these are not easy to obtain. Because of this lack of availability, the Cornish plays used to be thought to be curiosities of little dramatic interest.

However, new work on the Cornish plays, especially on the *Ordinalia*, has finally begun to do justice to their value as dramatic works of art. A new edition of *Origo Mundi*, the first play of the *Ordinalia* cycle, and a new translation of the *Ordinalia* have now been produced. The translation formed the basis of a production of the *Ordinalia* in Piran Round (one of the two surviving amphitheatres in Cornwall where some of the plays are thought to have been originally presented) by the Drama department of Bristol University in 1969. Earlier in the same year, part of *Meriasek* was produced by the same department in the Vandyke Theatre at Bristol University. Both productions were most successful, and the interest of these plays to a modern audience, as well as to scholars concerned with the early drama, has now been recognised.

This book hopes to show that the *Creacion* is an equally exciting piece of dramatic writing. It examines the structure and message of the play and reconsiders the evidence relating to its staging. New conclusions are drawn about its relationship to the earlier *Origo Mundi*, providing interesting additional information about the transmission of miracle plays in England, and about the role of the "English Pageant Master."

I would especially like to thank the following for their generous help: Oliver Padel, Place-names Research Fellow at the Institute of Cornish Studies in Truro, who has meticulously checked the text and translation and advised me about many details in the Introduction and Commentary; Ian Lancashire, Professor of English in Erindale College, Toronto, who read the whole of the MS most carefully and made numerous useful suggestions for improvement, and an anonymous publisher's adviser whose perceptive and detailed comments on the Introduction and translation have been invaluable.

I should also like to reiterate my thanks to the people who encouraged me when I first ventured into Cornish, particularly the late Phyllis Pier Harris of Everett Community College, Washington, and David Fowler and Markham Harris of the University of Washington in Seattle, for their hospitality and help. It will be apparent from the following pages how much I owe to their own work. The late Neville Denny of the University of Bristol read an early version of the Introduction and made some enlightening suggestions about staging; and John Leyerle supervised the Ph.D. thesis (Toronto, 1970) upon which the present book is based.

In addition, I should like to thank: Lord Bute for allowing me to examine the Keigwyn manuscript in his library and bringing it down to London for the purpose; Professor J. B. Trapp, Director of the Warburg Institute; Mr. Douch and Mr. Penhallurick of the library of the Royal Institution of Cornwall in Truro; the Canadian Commonwealth Scholarship Association, the University of Toronto, and the University of Kent at Canterbury, for grants towards the cost of research, and Birkbeck College for a grant towards the cost of reproducing the plates.

Parts of sections 1c and 1d of the Introduction originally appeared in a different form in articles in *Comparative Drama* and

Theatre Notebook, and I am grateful to the editors of these journals for permission to reprint copyright material. Also, for permission to reproduce plates: the British Library (plate 6), the Bodleian Library (plate 3), the Osterreichische National Bibliotek (plate 1), Charles Woolf (plates 2, 4, 5), and Roger Gilmour (plate 7).

Finally, I am most grateful to Barbara Brunswick and Sylvia Greenwood for their excellent typing and their patience.

Birkbeck College, London, 1980

List of Plates

Abbreviations

Allen D.C. Allen, *The Legend of Noah* (Urbana, 1963).

Anderson M.D. Anderson, *Drama and Imagery in English Medieval Churches* (Cambridge, 1963).

Boase and Courtney G.C. Boase and W.P. Courtney, *Bibliotheca Cornubiensis*, 3 vols. (London, 1874–82).

Carew Richard Carew, *Survey of Cornwall* (London, 1602).

Carey and Fowler *The Poems of John Milton*, ed. John Carey and Alastair Fowler (London, 1968).

Catholic Encyclopaedia Charles Herbermann, ed., *The Catholic Encyclopaedia*, 15 vols. (New York, 1907–14).

Cawley *The Wakefield Pageants in the Towneley cycle*, ed. A.C. Cawley (Manchester, 1958).

C-E-D R. Morton Nance, *A Cornish-English Dictionary* (Marazion, 1955).

Chambers E.K. Chambers, *The Mediaeval Stage*, 2 vols. (Oxford, 1903).

Chester *The Chester Mystery Cycle*, ed. R.M. Lumiansky and David Mills, Vol. 1 (London (EETS), 1974).

Coventry *Two Coventry Corpus Christi Plays*, ed. Hardin Craig (London (EETS), 1957).

Craig Hardin Craig, *English Religious Drama of the Middle Ages* (Oxford, 1955).

Creacion *The Creacion of the World: the first daie of playe.*

Cursor Mundi *Cursor Mundi*, ed. Richard Morris, Vol. 1 (London (EETS) 1874).

Dr. Faustus Christopher Marlowe, *Doctor Faustus*, ed. John D. Jump, Revels Plays (London, 1962).

ÉC *Etudes Celtiques.*

Emerson Oliver F. Emerson, "Legends of Cain, especially in Old and Middle English," *PMLA*, XXI (1906), pp. 831–930.

Everyman *Everyman*, ed. A.C. Cawley (Manchester, 1961).

Fowler David C. Fowler, "The Date of the Cornish 'Ordinalia,'" *Medieval Studies*, XXIII (1961), pp. 91–125.

Gwavas *Collections of William Gwavas on the Cornish Language*, British Library Add. MS 28, 554.

Holkham *The Holkham Bible Picture Book*, ed. W.O. Hassall (London, 1954).

Jenner Henry Jenner, *A Handbook of the Cornish Language* (London, 1904).

JRIC *Journal of the Royal Institution of Cornwall.*

Keigwyn Keigwyn's translation of *The Creacion of the World*, printed in *The Creation of the World, with Noah's Flood: written in Cornish in the year 1611, by William Jordan: with an English Translation by John Keigwyn*, ed. Davies Gilbert (London, 1827).

Kolve V.A. Kolve, *The Play Called Corpus Christi* (Stanford, 1966).

Lhuyd Edward Lhuyd, *Archaeologia Brittanica* (Oxford, 1707).

Macro *The Macro Plays*, ed. Mark Eccles (London (EETS) 1969).

"Memorial Reconstruction" Paula Neuss, "Memorial Reconstruction in a Cornish Miracle Play," *Comparative Drama*, V (1971), pp. 129–137.

Meriasek *Beunans Meriasek*, ed. Whitley Stokes, (London, 1872).

"N-town" *Ludus Coventriae or The Plaie called Corpus Christi*, ed. K.S. Block (London (EETS), 1922).

Nance *Gwryans an Bys*, ed. [R. Morton Nance and A.S.D. Smith. Marazion, 1959].

Non-Cycle Plays *Non-Cycle Plays and Fragments*, ed. Norman Davis (London (EETS) 1970).

Norris *The Ancient Cornish Drama*, ed. Edwin Norris, 2 vols. (Oxford, 1859).

ODCC *The Oxford Dictionary of the Christian Church*, ed. F.L. Cross (London, 1957).

OED *Oxford English Dictionary.*

OM *Origo Mundi*, first play of the *Ordinalia*, in Norris.

OMN *Origo Mundi*: First Play of the Cornish Mystery Cycle the *Ordinalia*, a New Edition, ed. Phyllis Pier Harris. (Unpublished Doctoral Dissertation, University of Washington, Seattle, 1964).

P "The Passion," ed. Whitley Stokes, *Transactions of the Philological Society*, [1] (1860–1), Appendix, pp. 1–100.

PC *Passio Christi*, second play of the *Ordinalia*, in Norris.

Piers Plowman *Langland's Vision of Piers the Plowman*, ed. W.W. Skeat (London (EETS) 1869; Pt. II, B-text, used unless otherwise stated).

PL *Patrologiae Cursus Completus*, series latina, ed. J-P Migne, 221 vols. (Paris, 1844–64)

"Plen an gwary" R. Morton Nance, "The Plen an gwary or Cornish playing-place," *JRIC* XXIV Pt. 3 (1935), pp. 190–211.

PMLA *Publications of the Modern Language Association.*

Pryce William Pryce, *Archaeologia Cornu-Brittanica* (Sherborne, 1790).

Quinn Esther C. Quinn, *The Quest of Seth for the Oil of Life* (Chicago, 1962).

RD *Resurrectio Domini*, third play of the *Ordinalia*, in Norris.

Robinson *The Works of Geoffrey Chaucer*, ed. F.N. Robinson, 2nd ed. (London, 1957).

Smith "The Commentary on *Gwryans an Bys*, or Jordan's *Creation of the World*, of A.S.D. Smith (Caradar)," ed. E.G.R. Hooper, *Cornish Studies* I (Camborne, 1962).

Southern Richard Southern, *The Medieval Theatre in the Round* (London, 1957).

Speculum humanae salvationis *Speculum humanae salvationis*, ed. J. Lutz et P. Perdrizet, 2 vols. (Mulhouse, 1907–9).

Stokes *Gwreans an Bys: The Creation of the World, a Cornish Mystery*, ed. Whitley Stokes (London, 1863; Berlin, 1864).

Tilley M.P. Tilley, *A Dictionary of the Proverbs in England in the Sixteenth and Seventeenth Centuries* (Ann Arbor, 1950).

Towneley *The Towneley Plays*, ed. G. England and A. Pollard (London (EETS), 1897).

VT *Le Mistère du Viel Testament*, ed. Baron James de Rothschild (Paris, 1878).

Wickham Glynne Wickham, *Early English Stages*, Vol. I (London, 1963).

Woolf Rosemary Woolf, *The English Mystery Plays* (London, 1972).

Young Karl Young, *The Drama of the Medieval Church*, 2 vols. (Oxford, 1933).

York *York Plays*, ed. L.T. Smith, 2nd ed. (New York, 1963).

Quotations from Chaucer are from Robinson; Shakespeare from the Arden editions; Milton from Carey and Fowler.

INTRODUCTION

1. The Play

a. 'a kind of Enterlude'

> The Guary miracle, in English, a miracle-play, is a kinde of Enterlude, compiled in *Cornish* out of some scripture history...

So Richard Carew begins his rather garbled account (given in full in Appendix 1) of the Cornish plays, in his *Survey of Cornwall,* printed in 1602. He was not very familiar with miracle plays, for they had ceased to be performed in the rest of the country.[1]

The Creacion of the World is the latest surviving example of a miracle-play in England. As well as being the last, it is certainly the least known, for reasons mentioned in the Preface. Yet it is by no means the least in terms of dramatic content. Because he put it together at the end of a long tradition of miracle-play composition, the playwright was able to make the best of the familiar material, and also to give it new life.

Our knowledge of the development of these plays in England is still somewhat hazy,[2] but it is generally accepted that by the end of the fourteenth century several cycles of plays dramatising biblical events from

1. See H.C. Gardiner, *Mysteries End,* New Haven, 1946.
2. See Woolf, Chapter IV, 'The Development of the Cycle Form' (pp. 54-76), for a useful account of the latest state of play.

the Creation of the World to the Last Judgment existed in England, of which four complete cycles and some fragments survive. On the Continent, however, the typical form of religious drama was not so much the historical cycle as the play on the life of Christ, focussing on the Passion. The fifteenth century Cornish cycle the *Ordinalia* is more of this type, the legend of the Cross-Tree being the basic unifying element of its structure.

The title-page of the *Creacion* states that it is *the first daie of playe,* which would seem to indicate that the play is intended to be the first day's portion of a full cycle similar in length to the *Ordinalia* (a cycle lasting three days) or possibly even longer than this, since the *Creacion* ends at the beginning of the Noah story, while *Origo Mundi* (the first play of the *Ordinalia* trilogy) covers all the Old Testament material of the cycle in about the same number of lines. At the end of the *Creacion,* as in the first two parts of the *Ordinalia*, the audience is told to 'come tomorrow on time' (2542) to see the next part of the cycle. No more of this supposed cycle than the *Creacion* survives, but the play does not seem incomplete. Unlike the English so-called 'non-cycle' plays, such as those of Norwich and Newcastle,[3] the *Creacion* has a unified

3. See *Non-Cycle Plays*, pp. 8-31.

structure and does not need to be part of any larger scheme. The movement of the play, from creation to destruction, is summed up by Noah, acting as chorus at the end:

> Why a wellas...
>   creacion oll an byse.
>
> In weth oll why a wellas
> An keth bysma consumys

('You have seen.../ ... the creation of all the world./ Also you have all seen/ the same world consumed' 2534-38)

The argument of the play centres on questions of life and death, good and evil, rather like a moral play. The figure of Death does not normally appear in these plays of biblical history (although he does arrive in the 'N-town' Death of Herod), nor does the audience usually get so much advice about how to regulate their own behaviour in the cycle plays, which are demonstrating history, as in the *Creacion*, where characters frequently give advice to the audience like preachers in moral plays. The playwright has worked on a small section of biblical history (some of it familiar to him through having acted in a version of *Origo Mundi*, see Section 1c below) turning it into a complete play in its own right, 'a kind of Enterlude', more like a moral play or moral interlude than a section of a cycle.

The *Creacion* dramatises events from the beginning of the world until Noah's flood, the beginning of the second age of man.[4] The main subject matter may be divided as follows:

The Creation of Heaven and the Angels, Fall of Lucifer	(1-335)
The Creation, Temptation, and Fall of Man	(336-962)
The Expulsion and coming of Death	(963-1053)
Cain and Abel	(1054-1391)
Seth's birth	(1392-1428)
Cain and Lamech	(1429-1725)
Seth's visit to Paradise and death of Adam	(1726-2094)
Translation of Enoch	(2095 2146)
The Making of the Pillars	(2147-2211)
Noah's Flood	(2212-2531)
Epilogue	(2532-2549)

4. Kolve argues that the theological tradition of the seven ages of man formed one of the principles for the selection of episodes in the cycle plays. Attractive as this view is, it seems to demand a necessity for greater emphasis on the Old Testament plays than is actually borne out by the existing cycles, and, as Kolve admits, 'no mediaeval cycle openly develops the theme' (p.99). However, this tradition might have been partly behind the *Creacion* writer's decision to end his play with Noah.

The structure of the *Creacion* is not shaped by these subjects, however, unlike that of some at least of the English cycles, where, particularly in the Old Testament material, each biblical episode forms a separate play or 'pageant'. The subject matter of the *Creacion* is fused together to form one continuous play. Although the scene constantly shifts between different sets of characters, figures used in one scene reappear later in another: Adam appears in the Creation and Fall scenes, before and after the Cain and Abel sequence, and before and after Seth's visit to Paradise; Seth appears in the scene of his birth after the murder of Abel, in the visit to Paradise after the murder of Cain, and in the making of the pillars after the death of Adam; Cain appears with Abel and then with Lamech; Death appears after the Expulsion from Paradise, and again after Seth's visit to Paradise, while God and Lucifer and the devils are inevitably involved in a number of scenes throughout the play. Having characters reappear in this manner creates an effect of continuous action in the play. The same characters do reappear in this manner in certain New Testament sections of the English cycles, those concerned with the life and Passion of Christ, and it could be argued that it is because the *Creacion* (like the *Ordinalia*) resembles the Continental Passion plays that it does have such continuity. But just as the *Creacion* with its presentation of Death and its constant insistence on the contrast and choice between good and evil is closer in tone to a moral play, even though its characters are *mainly* biblical rather than allegorical, so it seems to resemble a moral play in *form*.

The structure of the play is based upon shifts of scene rather than on biblical episodes, the episodes themselves being very much strung together. The open staging, using a *platea* and a number of different *loca* (see section 1d below), would naturally affect the structure of any play that was so presented, for in this method of staging, the action is continually moving from one part of the acting area to another. The playwright has used this shifting action to build up a series of contrasting scenes involving good and evil characters, in order to convey his didactic message dramatically. The actions of the good characters are set beside those of the bad: Abel beside Cain, Seth beside Lamech, Enoch against Tubalcain; those who obey God against the disobedient sinners. A chain of goodness is interwoven with a chain of evil, and the audience is invited to make its own comparison.

The good characters, Abel, Seth, Enoch, Noah, are traditionally grouped together because they are all types of Christ,[5] and the playwright makes a parallel

5. See *Glossa Ordinaria, PL* CXIII, 102, 103, 105, and, for a detailed study of typology, Jean Daniélou, *From Shadows to Reality: Studies in the Biblical Typology of the Fathers* (London, 1961).

association between his bad characters and the Devil. Lucifer is a *polat* (a curious word that seems literally to mean 'bighead'),[6] he calls himself *drog ('bad') pullat* (926), and is so called by Adam (770). Thus when the word is used of Lamech (1439), of Cain (1483) and of characters like Tubalcain and his friends (2355), connection with the Devil is implied, for the word is not used in the play except of these characters. Cain's association with Lucifer is made more strongly still, for Cain repeats some of the Devil's own words. Lucifer refuses to believe that God can forgive him:

> Nynges thymo remedy:
> An trespas ytho mar vras.
> Ny amownt whelas mercye;
> My a wore ny vyn an Tase
> Ow foly ȝymmo gava.

> ('There's no remedy for me; the sin was so great. It does no good to seek mercy; I know God won't forgive my folly', 426-30)

and Cain expresses his despair in similar words:

> Ow folly ythew mar vras,
> Haw holan in weth pur browt;
> Ny vanaf tha worth an Tase
> Whylas mercy, sure heb dowte,
> Kynnamboma lowena.

> ('My folly is so great, and my heart most proud too; I certainly won't seek mercy from God, although I'm unhappy', 1520-4)[7]

The good and bad characters, then, are linked together as types, as well as contrasted with their

6. See note on 141.
7. In *pur browt* (1521), and line 1524, Cain repeats other words of Lucifer's; see 271, 927. Cf. also 1364-5.

opposites, and in this there is nothing unusual for mediaeval drama. God sits in judgment over a series of tussles between the representatives of Christ and the Devil. But the structure of the *Creacion* is not one simply of contrasting types; there is a gradual change of emphasis as the play progresses. At the beginning, evil seems dramatically dominant, because the bad characters are more lively and interesting, but good has triumphed by the end. Naturally evil does not dominate at the very beginning of the play, where God reigns alone, and the question of good and evil does not arise, but almost as soon as the process of creation has begun, there is a division between good and evil, in the War in Heaven, and evil takes the dramatic foreground. Lucifer is the centre of the action and the audience cannot help admiring him, and then enjoying his jokes as Serpent. The sympathies of the audience gradually shift as the evil characters become duller and weaker by stages, till the good ones are seen in their true light. This is very similar to the movement we find in some of the moral plays, such as *Mankind* or *Magnificence,* where the audience tends at first to find the Virtues tedious, but is ultimately on their side. With Mankind - the human race - in the role of the Mankind or Everyman figure at the centre, the *Creacion* develops in a similar manner to these plays.

The evil characters move through a 'progressive

degradation' similar to that of Satan in *Paradise Lost*.[8] Lucifer is first seen as a bright angel, 'splanna es an howle' ('more splendid than the sun', 130), and although he loses his beauty when he falls, he manages to appear attractive by assuming the disguise of a virgin-faced serpent with yellow hair. As well as his pretty exterior he has a charming nature and a very appealing sense of humour. The charm is assumed for Eve's benefit, but the humour for that of the audience, who can appreciate, for example, the irony of his explanation to Eve that he has come from Heaven 'in a very great hurry' (557) to see her, and that she has no need to distrust him since 'only good people come from Heaven' (673). (This serpent has a far more interesting character than those of the English versions.) The compulsory nature of his departure from Heaven is not known to Eve as it is to the audience. Even when Lucifer is cursed by God after the Fall, and makes an undignified exit creeping *on his belly to Hell with great noyse* (917 sd.), he still seems to have the upper hand, for he points out that the 'chorle' Adam and his wife will be staying in Hell for ever, with their children, and the entrance of Death emphasises this.

However, Lucifer's undignified exit has literally reduced his stature in the eyes of the audience, and a

8. See C.S. Lewis, *A Preface to Paradise Lost* (Oxford, 1942), pp. 92-100.

process of degeneration has begun that is continued through Cain, the next representative of evil. Cain's comic behaviour tends to endear him to the audience to begin with. He is clever enough to deceive Adam with his false piety: 'It is essential, most essential, to toil/ and till the ground here' (1077-8), making use of a sententious phrase that is actually spoken by Adam himself in *Origo Mundi*, but adding an aside for only the audience to hear: '- to get ourselves food'. The audience must inevitably find Cain preferable to Abel, whose righteous indignation at Cain's intention to burn cowdung instead of his proper tithe is almost unbearable. Cain's wickedness, though, unlike that of Lucifer, is not strong enough to infect anyone else - Abel refuses to be tempted - and it also fails to profit himself. The smoke from Cain's offering will not burn properly, and this makes him look ridiculous. The audience probably had a sneaking sympathy with Cain's desire not to burn perfectly good food, but will soon change its mind when it sees the outcome. Cain's terror at the voice of Abel's blood crying out, and at God's curse, shows him up for the coward and bully he really is:

> *Let not Cayme looke in the Fatheris face, but look down and quake* (1164 sd.)

while the horns God sets on his head[9] make him ludicrous.

Lamech is the Devil's next representative, and his

9. See note on 1179 sd.

behaviour continues the degenerative process. Lamech admits to being a bully, which Cain had not done even if he was one, and he also announces that he is subject to lustful inclinations (he is the first bigamist and has many mistresses as well). The audience cannot extend to Lamech even the grudging admiration it felt for Cain at the beginning of the Cain and Abel sequence. The meeting of Cain and Lamech turns them both into buffoons: Cain, hairy and horned, looking like a wild man of the woods, has 'hidden' in a bush, but is perfectly visible to Lamech's boy:

> I see a very large animal
> squatting down in a bush (1514-5)

while Lamech gropes blindly about, unable to recognise his great-great-great-grandfather. Lamech's murder of his good-natured servant abolishes any sneaking sympathy that the audience might have had left for the sinners.

Lucifer is finally represented by the mockers of Noah, especially Tubalcain, who refuses to believe in the coming of the flood, and will not repent. Their taunting of Noah is stupid and insulting, yet Noah remains calm and unruffled, keeping his dignity. Unlike Jabel, the audience knows that God does want to drown the world - they have just seen Him say so - so there is no need for Noah to comment, except to suggest that the sinners mind their ways. The final joke at the expense of the wicked characters occurs when Tubal states that the making of the Ark is such a large task that it will never be finished, and Noah announces its completion in the very next line. Having laughed with Lucifer and Cain, and then at Cain and Lamech, the audience finds itself laughing behind the backs of Tubalcain and his friends.

Meanwhile, by a similar process, the good characters have been growing visibly stronger throughout the play. Humanity becomes utterly weak and helpless after the sin of Adam and Eve, and this is emphasised by their departure from the gates of Paradise, and the entry of the imposing figure of Death, which shows forcefully what God's creatures have brought upon themselves. Adam and Eve are left powerless, and can only lament the loss of Paradise. Like Mercy in *Mankind*, God retires from the action, leaving man on his own, with Death in the dramatic foreground, and the threat of Hell for ever. The audience has been emphatically shown the weakening effects of sin. A series of good and obedient characters seem, however, gradually to show that Paradise may be regained.

Abel is the first of these good characters, obedient to the wills of both his earthly and his Heavenly fathers, and his virtue is rewarded by God's acceptance of his offering. However, this is a brief triumph, for he is killed and thrown into a ditch. He is apparently not even carried off to Limbo, as Adam is, for no entrance for the devils is recorded, and it seems unlikely that they would have come in without speaking, when they make so much noise on other occasions. Abel probably crawls away out of sight after he is 'dead'. Goodness is not allowed much scope at this point in the play, and the audience's sympathies are with Cain. Abel is not even given the chance to retort to Cain's insults, as he does in *Origo Mundi*, where he calls his brother 'goky... ha mad' ('foolish and mad', *OM* 489), but answers all his taunts with meekness.

Seth, the next good character, is much stronger than Abel. The audience is told that he has the power to read the planets and foretell the future, which gives him an imposing mental stature, but more important dramatically, he is allowed to visit Paradise, and is rewarded by a vision of what is inside. This illustrates the growing strength of goodness, and shows the grace of God ready to reward the righteous. Adam and Eve had to leave Paradise, never to return. Seth is allowed to approach what they have lost, although he may not enter the gate. He takes back a message to Adam, and to all mankind, that salvation is possible.

The next type of obedience is Enoch, who, in reward for his virtue, is carried right *into* Paradise, while Seth had only been allowed as far as the gate. This shows the growing power of goodness as it gets closer to God, which is finally demonstrated when Noah is given the ability to build the Ark and survive the flood.

God supports those who obey Him, and goodness is admirable. Noah obtains the sympathies of the audience by the dignity of his behaviour, which contrasts with the sinners who mock him. It is probably because the dramatist wanted to protect Noah's dignity that the comic episode where Noah is beaten by his wife does not form part of the *Creacion* version of the Noah story, although there is a short comic passage concerning Mrs. Noah herself, who wishes to save some of her valuable property. In the *Creacion* Mrs. Noah is not allowed to get the better of Noah, as she does in some of the analogues.

Noah is given the last word in the play, and sums up what the audience has seen: creation and then destruction. Nobody has been spared, except Noah and his wife and children. The play has dramatised the chain of sin that leads from creation to destruction. A series of evil characters has been seen, and the play has emphasised that one sin leads inevitably to another: Satan's punishment for his sin leads him to tempt Eve; Adam sees Abel's death at the hands of Cain as a just punishment for his and Eve's sins; Lamech's killing of Cain is a just punishment for Cain's sins; Lamech and his sons must be punished sevenfold for Lamech's sins, and they are destroyed in the Flood. Evil, therefore, is caught in its own chain; it has destroyed itself, while good still survives.

The message, like that of any moral play, is commonplace enough, but it gains effectiveness through being conveyed through the dramatic shape of the play. Noah does not need to make any direct moral statement to sum up at the end, because the audience has seen the moral pointed up in the action.

b. Language and Imagery

The movement of the play is reinforced by a striking use of visual imagery. The most interesting example is the play's treatment of the device of the human-headed serpent in the Tree of Knowledge, a feature in the iconography of the Temptation usually assumed to have originated with Bede.[10] In the Temptation scene, Lucifer assumes the disguise of a serpent *with a virgyn face, and yolowe heare upon her head* (409 sd.), and sits in the Tree. The Serpent strongly resembles Eve in appearance (Bede had explained that that was how she could be so easily tempted). Eve resembles evil, and is dominated by it, as the Serpent sits above her in the Tree. Evil is visually, as well as morally, in the ascendant, at this point in the action. However, later in the play, when Seth is given his vision of Paradise, evil is subordinated, or made to appear grotesque, beside God. The Tree of Knowledge is dry and withered, and has

10. See note on 409 sd.

in its top the Serpent, whose virgin face is a grotesque parody of the face of the Virgin Mary, sitting in the top of the flourishing Tree of Life, with her child Jesus in her arms. The image is reminiscent of Milton's

> that only Tree
> Of Knowledge, planted by the Tree of Life;
> So near grows Death to Life
>
> (*Paradise Lost*, IV, 423-5)

but there Death dominates, while in the *Creacion* image life takes precedence. Although the image of the Serpent in the tree is common both in art and drama, the placing of the Virgin Mary in the Tree of Life is apparently peculiar to the *Creacion*.[11]

The use made of the figure of Death is also related to the movement of the play. Death appears after the Expulsion, personifying Genesis ii 17 'in the day that thou eatest thereof thou shalt surely die.'[12] He has complete power over Adam, and has been appointed by God to kill all the wicked with his dart. Nobody can escape Death. Later in the play, Death makes a second appearance, striking Adam with his dart. The audience sees Adam's body killed and buried, but his soul is taken to Limbo by an Angel: Death has no power over that.

11. See note on 1802 ff.
12. I quote from the Authorised Version throughout, since it is familiar, although, of course, the Vulgate would still have been used (see note on *a fowntayne*, 360 sd.).

The image of Hell is dealt with in a similar manner: its apparent power turns out to be weaker than the audience had thought at first. This may be seen by contrasting the scenes of the death of Cain and the death of Adam, visually very similar to begin with. On both occasions, the devils come bursting triumphantly out of Hell to carry off the dead. The difference is that while they succeed with Cain:

The devills careth them with great noyse to Hell (1720 sd.)

they return empty-handed after the death of Adam:

They go to Hell with great noyes (2064 sd.)

The *noyes* turns out to be a fuss about nothing, and Hell's gaping mouth looks a little foolish. The later scene had looked to be a repetition of the earlier, but turned out differently: the devils are unable to take Adam to Hell, as they had Cain. Adam has repented, and will therefore go to Limbo, where the devils cannot touch him, to wait for the Harrowing of Hell, when he can get to Heaven. The explanation about the difference between Hell and Limbo (2020 ff.) seems deliberately reserved until late in the play, so as not to detract from the apparently helpless position of mankind after the Fall, when there was no end in view but death and Hell. The audience had been inclined to admire Cain's bravado in continually refusing to repent and now the consequences of this rash pride become clear:

Cain goes to Hell, whereas Adam, who *has* repented, is taken to Limbo. The audience can see, too, how Lucifer has fallen. He had triumphantly expected Adam and his offspring to remain in Hell for ever, and now he is forced to explain that they won't. The devils had expected the death of Adam to be a repetition of that of Cain, but it turns out differently from what they had anticipated.

Repetition or near-repetition is sometimes used in the dialogue with a similarly ironic effect. God, for example, consciously echoes Lucifer's own boast 'Me ew lantorn Nef' (123), in his condemnation of the Devil when he falls: 'Ty a ve oll lantorn Nef' (228); Eve unconsciously echoes words Lucifer has spoken several times to her when she tells Adam: 'A vell Dew ny a vea,/ Ha maga fure' ('we would be like God,/ and as wise', 782-3); Noah consciously repeats the request of Tubal to tell him 'der vanar da' ('in a nice manner', 2334), what is the trouble, when he tells Tubal: 'if you will be repentent,/*in* a nice manner, then/this same punishment will pass away', (2344-6); Lucifer's words when he hears that man has been made to take his place are unconsciously repeated by Cain when he speaks of Abel's desire to burn the corn (cf. 440 and 1129).

Repetition is used for other purposes in the dialogue as well. Its use for linking together the bad characters, especially Lucifer and Cain, has already been discussed. Repetition is used also to emphasise a point that needs bringing home to the audience, such as that Cain continually refuses to repent, or that God can, if he wishes, destroy his creation in a word, just as he formed it.

The effect of Seth's repeated description of Paradise, and the marvels it contains, given firstly to the Cherub and then to Adam, is to provide a poignant reminder of what Adam has lost, and how he can no longer see Paradise for himself, as well as to indicate what joys are in store for the virtuous. Occasionally, it is true, the repetition becomes somewhat excessive: a point is given more emphasis than it seems to need. This is most noticeable in connection with the mark God sets on Cain, his reasons for doing so, and what he said when he did it. Firstly, the scene itself is enacted; it is then reported by Cain's wife, Calmana (and how did she know about it?); next we hear the story from Cain himself, when he reappears in exile; and finally, Cain explains the situation to Lamech. Even allowing for some comic by-play in connection with this 'mark', a pair of horns, the quadruple repetition seems unnecessarily tedious. Cornish drama does occasionally have this fault; in the doubting of Thomas scene in *Resurrectio Domini* (the third play of the *Ordinalia*), each of the other disciples tries twice to persuade Thomas that Christ has risen, and the scene lasts for about 700 lines! However, the English moral interludes are not always restrained in their messages either, and verbal repetition is normally used skilfully in the *Creacion*, like the visual images.

Besides the use of repetition, one of the most interesting features of the language of the *Creacion* is its offsetting of the English and Cornish languages, for it often uses English for low characters, while God 'invariably speaks pure Cornish'.[13] Two of Lucifer's speeches contain several consecutive lines of English (see note on 113), while Cain and Lamech use English too, and sometimes when the Devil repeats something God has said, he replaces a Cornish word by an 'English' one (see e.g. notes on 444, 464). This produces an effect similar to the high and low style of the English moral plays, where the Latinate diction of the Virtues contrasts with the 'plain-speaking' of the Vices.

The playwright also sometimes makes deliberate use of bilingual puns, particularly in the Temptation scene. Lucifer says he will 'prevent' Adam (494), punning on *preve* ('serpent'), and that he will go *prevathe*, 505, ('privately' and 'like a *preve*') to Paradise. Perhaps sometimes apparent 'puns' are coincidental, for example, the reference to God's creating the world *orth compas* 'in due proportion' and

13. Fowler, p. 111.

'with a compass' (see note on 19) and the 'voice' that cries out, of Abel's blood (see note on 1153),[14] but Lucifer's puns are quite in character, suitable for a fellow so skilled in irony.

c. Relationship to 'Origo Mundi'

The *Creacion* has usually been thought to be an imitation and expansion of the opening part of the *Ordinalia*. Stokes noted that 'the author imitates and often copies the *ordinale* called 'Origo Mundi'' (p.4); Jenner said that 'the author has borrowed whole passages from it [*Origo Mundi*], and there are many additions to the story in it, and much amplification of the ideas and dialogue', (p. 31); Chambers described the play as an 'expansion of part of the earlier text'.[15]

However, a careful examination of the texts of the two plays shows that these are hardly accurate descriptions of the relationship of the later play to the earlier. The section of the *Ordinalia* concerned is the first 1257 lines of *Origo Mundi*. This section (less than half the play) occupies folios 1r-11v in the surviving manuscript (MS. Bodley 791) and deals with

14. In 'Memorial Reconstruction' I suggested that the writer had misrepresented the Cornish in these cases because he was thinking of their English homophones, but I now see that this is an over-simplification.
15. Chambers, II, p. 125.

Biblical events from the Creation of the World to Noah's Flood. The whole of the *Creacion* also covers events up to and including the Flood: a whole day is given in the later play to dramatising events occupying less than half the earlier one. This fact alone could lead to describing the later play as an 'expansion'. The *Creacion* contains much subject-matter that does not appear at all in *Origo Mundi*: the Creation of the Angels; the Fall of Lucifer[16]; the coming of Death after the Fall; Cain's death at the hands of Lamech; the Translation of Enoch; the making of the pillars of brick and marble by Seth and Jared.

However, a comparison of material that does appear in both plays shows that there are some very striking similarities between the two. A number of lines and passages (including two speeches of sixteen lines and one of twenty-four) in the early part of *Origo Mundi* are repeated almost verbatim in the *Creacion*, except that they show the spelling changes and the occasional substituting of an 'English' word for a Cornish one that are typical of late mediaeval Cornish. One example will suffice. The *Origo Mundi* lines

> Adam saf yn ban yn clor
> ha treyl the gyk ha the woys
> preder me the'th whul a dor
> haval they'm a'n pen the'n troys
> myns us yn tyr hag yn mor
> warnethe kemer galloys
> yn bysma rak dry ascor
> ty a vew bys may fy loys (65-72)

16. There are stage directions in *Origo Mundi* referring to the Fall of Lucifer, however; at *OM* 49 and 148 (the latter deleted by the scribe).

appear thus in the *Creacion:*

Adam, save in ban in cloer,
Ha trayle ȝa gyke hatha owg.
Predar me thath wrill a thoer,
Havall ȝym then pen ha tros.

Myns es in tyre hag in moer,
Warnothans kymar gallus.
Yn serten, rag dry ascore,
Ty a vew may fota loose. (352-59)

The only difference in translation derives from the substitution of *yn sertan* ('certainly') in the *Creacion* for *yn bysma* ('in this world, here') in *Origo Mundi.* Such 'identical' lines, though, are not as great in number as has often been assumed.[17] Only 183 of the 1257 lines in the *Origo Mundi* section are repeated among the 2549 of the *Creacion.* A closer look at these lines and the scenes in which they occur leads to some interesting conclusions about the relationship of certain parts of the *Creacion* to *Origo Mundi.*

The 'identical' lines (see Appendix II) occur in only three episodes in the plays: the Creation and Fall; the Cursing of Cain; and the Noah sequence. More significantly, of the 183 lines, 132 are among the speeches of one character, God the Father. These include all the repeated passages of more than 4 lines (except one speech by Adam) and two passages of 16 lines

17. This was first noted by Phyllis Pier Harris in the edition of *Origo Mundi* (as yet unpublished) which was her Doctoral Dissertation for the University of Washington (Seattle, 1964).

and one of 24. The remaining lines are spoken by characters as follows: Adam, 26; Cain, 9 (one of which belongs to Adam in *OM*); Serpent, 6; Cherub, 6; Noah, 4 (2 of which belong to Cain, and 1 to Epilogue, in *OM*). Many of these lines spoken by characters other than God occur in *Origo Mundi* (though not always in the *Creacion*) either immediately before, or immediately after, speeches spoken by God that are repeated in the *Creacion*. In other words, when a speech by God from *Origo Mundi* is repeated in the *Creacion*, lines spoken before and after it tend to be repeated too. This evidence seems to suggest that the compiler of the *Creacion* had access to some of the lines of an actor who had played God in *Origo Mundi*: some of his speeches and cues.

There is evidence that actors' parts in medieval plays were sometimes written down separately, as in the surviving *Dux Moraud*, Shrewsbury, and *Processus Satanae* fragments, the last being the part of God the Father from an English miracle play, with his cues.[18] However, several considerations make it seem unlikely that the compiler of the *Creacion* had access to such a written copy, even if one can be supposed to have existed, although the curious appearance of a Latin speech-heading, *Deus Pater*, at line 336 of the *Creacion* (just before the first speech of God's repeated from *Origo*

18. See W.W. Greg, *Dramatic Documents from the Elizabethan Playhouses* (Oxford, 1931), I, pp. 173-75.

Mundi) might be taken as evidence of this. (See plate 3. *Origo Mundi* uses this heading for God throughout, and all the other speech-headings in the *Creacion* are in English.) The differences in spelling suggest that the *Creacion* compiler was unlikely to have been using a *written* actor's part from *Origo Mundi*. But more important is the fact that there are lines from *Origo Mundi* repeated in the *Creacion* that are not God's cue lines in the earlier play and would therefore be unlikely to appear in a written copy of God's part (at least from *Origo Mundi* as we now have it). They do, however, all occur in scenes where God is present. An actor would certainly remember scattered lines from parts other than his own. There are no repetitions of more than three consecutive lines among these 'non-cue' lines; mostly they are single lines or couplets. Some are even assigned to different speakers from the original characters. Eg. in *Origo Mundi*, after the birth of Seth, Adam says:

> rys yw porrys lafurrye
> ('It is necessary, most necessary, to work', 683)

but in the *Creacion* this is spoken ironically by Cain as he goes to sacrifice on Mount Tabor. There may be no significance in this at all (the line is a *sententia* and the 'repetition' may be coincidence), but it is possible that the compiler intended extra irony in having Cain use one of Adam's devout speeches. Or else the actor may simply have remembered the line without its context, and found it useful to insert at this point. Anyway the existence of these 'non-cue' lines seems to point more towards the use of a reported text than of a written actor's part, suggesting a memorial reconstruction of part of the play by an actor who had played the part of God the Father in *Origo Mundi*.

In addition to the repeated lines, there are other aspects of the *Creacion* text that suggest it may have been at least partly reconstructed from memory. Certain lines in the three scenes where actual repetition occurs show near-repetition or paraphrasing of other of the *Origo Mundi* lines, as if the actor could only remember the original lines imperfectly at some points.

For example, compare the two accounts given by Eve as to how she obtained the apple:

My pan esen ov quandre
    clewys a'n nyl tenewen
vn el ov talleth cane
    a vghaf war an wethen

(*OM*, 213-6)

Sera, ha me ow *qwandra*,
Me a glowas a wartha
War an weathan udn eal wheake
Sure *ow cana*.

(*Creacion*, 758-61)

And Adam's reply:

A out warnes drok venen
    worto pan wrussys cole
rag ef o tebel ethen
    neb a glewsys ov cane

(*OM*, 221-24)

A, Eva, Eva, ty a fyllas,
Ow cola orthe an eal na.
Droke polat *o*, me a gryes,
Neb a glowses owe cana.

(*Creacion*, 768-71)

Part of Cain's reply to God after the death of Abel is repeated verbatim in the *Creacion*, and part of the remainder is a paraphrase of the *Origo Mundi* lines. For example:

ellas my a wor henna
bones ov fegh moy yn-ta
    es mercy dew.

(*OM*, 590-2)

Moy ew ow gwan oberowe
Hag in wethe *ow fehosowe*
Es tell ew tha *vercy, Dew,*
Thym tha ava.

(*Creacion*, 1167-70)

The italicized words in the *Creacion* sections show repetition or near-repetition of those in *Origo Mundi*, and the verses are filled out either with phrases such as *sure, me a gryes*, 'certainly', 'I believe', or, as in the last example, by doubling the nouns - both features typical of the style of the *Creacion* play as a whole. Such 'paraphrasing' lines occur only in the scenes in the *Creacion* similar to those in *Origo Mundi where God is present*, and it is important to notice that although there are other scenes in the two plays dealing with the same subject matter, such as the Seth sections, there are no echoes in the *Creacion* of the *Origo Mundi* words in these sections. *God was not needed for these scenes*. In fact God the Father takes little active part in events after the Flood, which *may* explain why the *Creacion* concludes at this point.

The existence of these 'paraphrasing' lines is further support for a theory of memorial reconstruction of at least part of the *Creacion* text. If this assumption is correct, then we have in the *Creacion* text something resembling the 'bad' quartos of Shakespeare, though without the stigma attached to these, since there was no question of individual authorship for a miracle play. In fact these details may shed light on some aspects of *Origo Mundi* itself. The duplication of certain lines in that play,[19] as well as the references in the stage directions to Lucifer scenes not appearing in the text, are indications that the *Origo Mundi* text itself is probably put together from a source or sources that may have been partly verbal. Not enough is known about the transmission of miracle plays; the close similarity between some of the plays in the York

19. Eg. God's speech regretting the creation of man occurs at *OM* 417-21, 423 and *OM* 917-22; Adam and Noah are tired in the same way 684-5 and 1009, 1013.

and Towneley cycles has not been throughly examined and explained, for instance.

This evidence about the construction of part of the *Creacion* text of course still leaves much of the play unaccounted for - all except the three sections of the Creation and Fall, Cursing of Cain, and Noah's Flood - and there seems no way of knowing whether the rest of the play was put together in a similar manner. A comparison of the treatment of other material in the two plays shows that *Origo Mundi* is unlikely to have been a source for many parts of the *Creacion* other than these three scenes, so the theory that *Creacion* is merely an expansion of *Origo Mundi* is not valid. Some of the *Origo Mundi* episodes are omitted in the *Creacion:* it deals with the naming of the animals much more briefly than *Origo Mundi;* it omits the scene where the earth will not allow Adam to dig it, the blessing of Abel by his parents, and the seraph who tells Adam and Eve that they are to have another child. The main material that appears in both plays, other than the three scenes where duplication occurs, is the Seth story, and the form of this differs quite considerably in the two versions. In *Origo Mundi* (as in most versions) Seth is given three separate glimpses of Paradise: first he sees the garden with the fountain and the dry tree; then the Serpent in the dry tree; and finally the child in the green tree. The tree is apparently the same one in each vision. In the *Creacion*, Seth has only one vision, in which he sees two trees, the dry tree with the Serpent, and the green tree, identified as the Tree of Life, with the Virgin Mary, and the child, identified as Jesus, and Cain in Hell. He does not refer to the fountain (although there is one in Paradise at the beginning of the *Creacion*, in the Creation scene, where *Origo Mundi does* seem to be a source). Another minor difference is that when Adam dies, Seth places the pips between his teeth and his tongue in *Origo Mundi*, and in his mouth and nostrils in the *Creacion*.

Further differences are that in *Origo Mundi* devils enter and carry off Adam and Abel to Hell, while in the *Creacion*, Cain is taken to Hell, Adam goes to Limbo, and Abel seems to be left in a ditch; in the scene between Noah and his wife (part of the Noah episode where God is not 'on stage'), Mrs. Noah is humbly obedient in *Origo Mundi*, while in the *Creacion* she is treated slightly comically.

Some of these differences in treatment, however, may be conscious alterations by the dramatist, in accordance with his intention in the play, and need not necessarily militate against *Origo Mundi* as a source for the episodes the plays have in common, even if the relationship is not as intimate as that for the three scenes where lines are duplicated. But since *Origo Mundi* itself is probably not original, it looks as if the relationship between the two plays is more like that of uncle to niece than of parent to child, and there may be a putative 'uhr-cycle' behind both.

The existence of the Creation window of St. Neot Church in Cornwall (see plate 2) might be further evidence for this 'uhr-cycle', for it is obviously earlier in date than our play (1480-1530) and yet has some of the same material, not all of which is to be found in *Origo Mundi*.

Like the *Creacion*, it depicts a series of episodes from the creating of the world to the life of Noah, although its last panel shows only the building of the Ark, and the Flood is reserved for the next (later) window. The material covered in the Creation window includes: the creating of the angelic orders; the Creation and Fall of Man; the Expulsion; Cain and Abel; Cain and Lamech; the Death of Adam (including Seth's placing of the pips in his mouth); and the building of the Ark.

The *Creacion* contains many episodes not shown in this window, but there are some correspondences in treatment of the common material. In both cases there are ten orders of angels rather than nine; in the first panel of the window God is seen creating the world with a pair of compasses (see note on 19); the serpent in panel five has a human head and yellow hair (see plate 4); Adam and Eve are shown with a spade and distaff after the Expulsion; Cain's smoke is shown blowing downwards while Abel's rises to Heaven (see note on 1091); Abel is killed with a jawbone; Cain appears to have horns (see note on 1179 sd.); Adam is shown in bed (see plate 5 and note on 1999 sd.).

Most of these correspondences are admittedly not surprising, for many of these details (the compass, the human-headed serpent, the spade and distaff, the 'bush of smoke', the jawbone) were devices and props that seem to have been commonly used in productions of miracle plays, although most plays do not leave such a clear indication as does the *Creacion* with its abundance of stage directions. But there are some unusual parallels, notably the depiction of Cain with horns and Adam in bed, neither apparently found elsewhere in art or drama. It is not very likely that the playwright would have included these details simply through having seen them at St. Neot (and in any case Cain's horns there are more like antlers, and nothing like the ω or bullock's horns that Cain has in the *Creacion*). Probably these elements in both the Creation window and the *Creacion* are derived from things recalled from an earlier production, which could not be the *Ordinalia* as we have it, since it apparently does not include a horned Cain or a bedded Adam (these elements *might* have appeared in the staging, but it is unlikely, since there is no reference to them in the text), and was probably a production of my postulated 'uhr-cycle', the parent version of the *Ordinalia* that survives, from which the Creation window and the *Creacion* also derive.[20] The Cornishman Trevisa's insertion of books into the pillars made before the Flood in his translation of Higden's *Polychronicon* (see note on 2181 ff.) may also derive from something seen in such a production.

20. This 'uhr-cycle' itself would of course derive ultimately from the Vulgate, *via* the patristic commentaries. The *Creacion* also has a similar range of material to the opening part of the fifteenth-century French cycle *Le Mistère du Viel Testament* (although the *VT* has even more episodes, such as debates between Justice and Mercy, and the Death of Eve, and many more characters). But in spite of the editor's claim that the *Creacion* 'se rapproche... de notre grand drame' (p. xlviii) there seem to be no lines or passages that suggest a translation or paraphrase of the French into Cornish, and both plays could have derived their subject matter independently from the *Historia Scholastica* or some similar source. The later Breton Creation play ('La Creation du Monde: Mystère Breton', ed. E. Bernard, *RC*, IX, pp.149-207, 322-353; X, 192-211, 414-455; XI, 254-317) is analogous to the *Creacion* in its selection of episodes, but contains even more material, taking two days to reach the Flood. In spite of the editor's suggestion that the two plays derive from the source, the material and presentation are really quite different. For instance the naming of the animals takes over 100 lines in the Breton!

d. <u>Staging</u>

One of the most interesting aspects of the *Creacion* is the fullness of its stage directions - they are much fuller than those of the other Cornish plays or than anything in the English cycles except perhaps the *Ludus Coventriae* Passion plays. The stage directions are all in English, and seem to fall into two main types: either authorial instructions to the actors, e.g.: *Lett Eva looke stranglye on the Serpent when she speakethe* (552 sd.); *Let Tuball fall a laughing* (2299 sd.); and on the design of the sets, e.g.: *Let Paradice be fynelye made, with two fayre trees in yt. . .* (359 sd.); *Two pyllars made, the on of brick and thother of marbell* (2186 sd.); or what seem to be prompt-copy instructions to or from the stage-manager: *Fig leaves redy to cover ther members* (870 sd.); *A lamb redy with fyre and insence* (1079 sd.); *A chawbone readye* (1109 sd.).

The manuscript of the *Creacion* contains no diagram or staging plan, unlike those of the other Cornish plays.[21] Nevertheless it has usually been assumed that its method of staging would have been similar to theirs, that is, playing in the round, in an open amphitheatre, in the manner Carew described:

21. These plans are reproduced in Norris, Vol. I, pp. 219, 479; Vol. II, p.200; and (in diagram form) *Meriasek* pp. 144, 266.

> For representing it [the Guary miracle], they raise an earthen Amphitheatre, in some open field, having the Diameter of his enclosed playne some 40. or 50. foot.
>
> (p.71)

Two amphitheatres exist in Cornwall today, at St. Just-in Penwith and Perranzabuloe. These are the only remaining examples of the *plen-an-guary* or 'playing-place'[22] which Carew seems to be describing. That the *Ordinalia* was intended for performance in such a round seems proven not only by the three diagrams in the manuscript, but also by the success of the production of it in Piran Round by Bristol University Drama Department in 1969.

Southern suggests that the world *playne* which occurs twice in the *Creacion* stage directions (326 sd., 488 sd.) is used in the same sense as *place* or *platea* in the other Cornish plays and in *The Castle of Perseverance*, and that this implies use of the same kind of staging, that the play was performed in the round.[23] However, although the word is the same as that used by Carew, there is no evidence that I can find in the *Creacion* that this *playne* was 'enclosed' in the manner Carew described and which is indicated in

22. See 'Plen an Gwary' for a description of these rounds and a list of places in Cornwall where others may have existed.
23. Southern, p.225. The playwright (or scribe) of the *Creacion* seems to confuse the two words at one point; see note on 2269-70.

the diagrams of the other Cornish plays. The surviving diagrams for 'theatre-in-the-round' all show a number of stations or mansions grouped round the *place*; eight in each of the three days of the *Ordinalia*, thirteen in both days of *Meriasek*, and five in the *Castle*. The *Creacion*, however, seems to have had only three stations: Heaven, Hell, and Paradise.

The structures of Heaven and Hell were clearly extremely elaborate. It appears from the scene in which the angels are created that Heaven may have had three tiers or levels. The first level contained God's throne, and that this was higher than other parts of Heaven can be seen from the directions *Let hem* [Lucifer] *offer to assend to the trone* (194 sd.), and *Let Lucyfer offer to go upe to the trone* (313 sd.), both of which occur while Lucifer is still in Heaven. There are three degrees of angels: the first three 'next [or, nearest] to my throne' (37); 'the second degree' (51), which is probably lower; 'the third degree below' (59). The ordering of the angels is one of status, and may not have been represented physically, but Heaven must have had at least two levels including that containing the throne. There are three concentric circles in Heaven in the Cailleau miniature of the Valenciennes Passion play, and in the Fouquet miniature of the martyrdom of St. Apollonia the angels in Heaven appear to be arranged in tiers.[24] In the *Creacion* these levels were possibly also divided into sections or special places for each kind of angel. In the direction for the War in Heaven: *All Angells must... com to the rome wher Lucyfer ys* (300 sd.), though *rome* may mean simply 'space, area' (*OED* room *sb.*[1] 5), its meaning may be closer to the usual modern sense. In 2258 *rowmys* clearly means 'rooms' (or cabins), for it refers there to the living quarters of the Ark, the *mansiunculas* of the Vulgate. Each angel may have had his own special *rome*, space or position (cf. *OED* room, sb.[1] 5e 'square... on a chessboard').[25] One is reminded of Archdeacon Rogers' description (written in 1609) of the Chester pageant-houses: 'a highe place made like a howse with ij rowmes'.[26] An interesting point is that if Heaven were so constructed, with three levels divided into sections, it would closely resemble the Ark with its 'thre chese chambres', as the Towneley play describes it, its three rows of living quarters. This would make an excellent visual

24. See e.g. A.M. Nagler, *The Medieval Religious Stage* (London, 1976), p.85 and frontispiece.
25. Cf. *Speculum humanae salvationis*, plate 127, where the angels are shown arranged in a dyptych, with ten squares each side.
26. Quoted e.g. in F.J. Furnivall, ed., *The Digby Plays* (London (EETS), 1896), p.xix. Rogers thought that the lower *rowme* was a kind of tiring-house. Chambers (II, p. 135) said that *rome* in the *Creacion* meant one of the stations, but this is impossible, for the fight in Lucifer's *rome* takes place in Heaven.

association, for Augustine had laid down that the Ark signified the Church.[27]

The station for Hell appears to have had two levels: the *pytt*, which is 'below' (2034), and the *clowster*, 'cloisters' (2027), or *Lymbo*, which is 'up above' (2018). The direction *Lett hell gape when the Father nameth yt* (245 sd.) shows that the *pytt* was a Hell-mouth, and Hell was commonly so represented on the mediaeval stage. The structure used in the *Creacion* must have resembled that of the Digby Mary Magdalen play, where Lucifer enters *In a stage, and Helle ondyr-neth þat stage*,[28] and also those in the Valenciennes and Fouquet miniatures, both of which have two levels, the lower being a Hell-mouth.

Hell is also referred to as 'the kitchen' (2013) and probably a large cooking-pot was part of its design, as it was in the illustration of the Last Judgement in *The Holkham Bible Picture Book* (see plate 6). There seems to be a cooking-pot containing souls inside the Valenciennes Hell-mouth, too. Cauldrons symbolise Hell in *The Croxton Play of the Sacrament* and *The Jew of Malta*; the Chester Harrowing of Hell is presented appropriately by the Cooks and

27. See Kolve, p.69.
28. Furnivall, *op cit.*, p.67, l. 357 sd.

Innkeepers, while in the *Jeu d'Adam* devils are instructed to 'dash together their pots and kettles.'[29] The devils in *Resurrectio Domini* announce:

> We will die making a fire
> Under the kettle.
> Drink, there are with me
> More than a million souls
> In a very fair broth.
>
> (*RD*, 138-42)[30]

'The kitchen' seems sometimes to be a euphemism for Hell in Cornish expletives, and this may have arisen through its stage presentation.[31]

Paradise was perhaps less elaborate than Heaven and Hell, though it was *fynelye made*, as the direction at 350 shows, and it contained, besides the two trees, *a fowntayne... and fyne flowres in yt paynted* (359 sd.). It must have been quite large, for in the Fall scene it contained both Eve and the Serpent, and Adam some distance away.

29. Quoted e.g. in A.M. Nagler, *A Source Book in Theatrical History* (New York, 1959), p. 47.
30. 'During the quarrel between Beelzebub and Lucifer a demon named Tulfric makes some remarks that I do not fully understand, but they clearly intimate he is concerned in some way in the *cooking of souls*' (Thurstan Peter, *The Old Cornish Drama* (London, 1906), p.30).
31. Jenner remarks however: 'Another serio-comic but rather cryptic expletive, peculiar to Camborne, or at any rate to the Drama of *St. Meriasek*, is *Mollath Dew en gegin*! God's curse in the kitchen! It does not seem to mean anything in particular, except perhaps that one's food may not agree with one (p. 55).

No other *loca* are mentioned in the stage directions, but it might be thought that the speech-heading *Lamech in tent* (1429) points to the existence of at least one other station, for these are sometimes called *tenti* (otherwise *pulpita*) in the stage directions of the *Ordinalia.* In *Passio Christi,* for instance, there are references in the directions to the *tenti* of Pilate, Herod, and Cayphas (454 sd., 1573 sd., 1616 sd., 1687 sd., 1882 sd., 1934 sd., 2066 sd.). These are all names that appear on the perimeter of the circular diagram for that day, or round the edge, apparently, of the amphitheatre. A similar position might therefore be deduced for Lamech's *tent* in the *Creacion*, and if he had one, other characters may have done too, although no other actors' stations are mentioned. Lamech's first words are similar to those of Enoch and Noah; they all declare their names somewhat in the manner of the characters in the *Ordinalia* who parade on their scaffolds. As Lamech speaks first *in tent*, possibly Enoch and Noah had *tenti* too.

However, these figures are not major characters like those who have their own *tenti* in the *Ordinalia.* Noah does not have one in *Origo Mundi*, and he is no more important a character in the *Creacion.* I believe that Lamech is the only character in the *Creacion* who had a *tent*, and that it was not a curtained booth on a raised platform like the *tenti* of the *Ordinalia*, but a literal tent with an iconographic significance. Lamech was thought to be the inventor of tents:

> hit is kynde of man,
> Sith Lamek was, that is so longe agoon,
> To ben in love as fals as evere he can;
> He was the firste fader that began
> To loven two, and was in bigamye;
> And *he found tentes first, but yf men lye.*
>
> (*Anelida and Arcite*, 149-54)

Robinson comments: 'It is really Jabal, Lamech's son, who is called 'the father of such as dwell in tents', referring to Genesis iv, 19-20.[32] Lamech's tent in the *Creacion* draws attention to what was thought to be an aspect of his character. I believe it to have been a moveable property like the Ark, and not a fixed station. If it had been present throughout the entire action, like the *tenti* in the *Ordinalia*, it could not have had any iconographic significance.

So there seem to have been only three fixed stations, hardly enough to constitute a 'round'. Moreover, the stations in the other Cornish plays and the *Castle* were raised, for actors had to go up to them and down from them. But the only references in the *Creacion* to ascending or descending are made in connection with Heaven: God descends to the earth (74-5); *Lucyfer... goeth downe to Hell* [from Heaven] (326 sd.); *Let the Father assend to Heaven* (953 sd.); *Desend Angell* (971 sd.). Heaven, then, was a raised

32. Robinson, p. 790.

station of some kind. There is nothing, however to suggest that Hell and Paradise were not on the same level as the rest of the action, nor, supposing Lamech's *tent were* a fixed station, does he make any mention of ascending or descending, unlike the characters with *tenti* in the *Passio Domini*. If Lamech's *tent* were on the edge of an amphitheatre, one would expect him to *go down* into the *place*. If the stations were not raised it is most unlikely that they would have been arranged in the round, since it would then have been very difficult for the audience to see the action.

The stations could, of course, all have been in the *place*, like the Castle in the *Castle*, and Meriasek's chapel. But in the diagrams for these plays only the one *locus* is shown in the *place*, and sight lines would have been obscured if there had been more. The person who drew the *Castle* diagram was concerned about *lettynge of syt* as it was, with the Castle in the middle of the place.[33] The *Creacion* stations were obviously quite substantial, and also there are a number of other items of scenery besides Heaven, Hell and Paradise that would have to be in the *place* for part of the action: Mount Tabor, the bush in which Cain hides, the forest (1491 sd.), Adam's bed and his tomb, the Ark, as well as Lamech's tent. Admittedly some

33. See Southern, p. 72 ff.

of these might have been natural features of the *place*,[34] such as the bush and the forest (if it was not too large). Mount Tabor (which might be specially built from a heap of earth, leaving a ditch in which Cain could throw Abel's body (1136 sd.)[35] may have been quite small. But still the *place* would have been extremely cluttered if the stations were in it. And this in any case would not conform to the usual conception of 'theatre-in-the-round', which has the stations surrounding the *place*.

The *Creacion* was not staged then, in quite the same way as the other Cornish plays seem to have been, for Heaven is the only raised station, and there are not many other *loca* mentioned. Most of the action apparently took place in the *playne*. This may not have been circular, but possibly semi-circular or even oblong, with the stations arranged in a line or semi-circle behind it, and the audience in front: the kind of arrangement that is shown in the miniature of the manuscript of the Valenciennes Passion play, where

34. The production of Lyndsay's *Ane Satyre of the Thrie Estaitis* at Cupar, for instance, took advantage of natural features of the area. See Glynne Wickham, 'The Staging of Saints Plays in England', in Sandro Sticca ed., *The Medieval Drama* (Albany, 1972), pp.114-5.
35. Cf. Southern's view that a mound was thrown up when the ditch in the *Castle* was dug (pp.50-56). However, Natalie C. Schmitt ('Was there a Medieval Theatre in the Round? A Re-examination of the evidence', *Theatre Notebook*, XXIII (1968-9), pp. 130-42; XXIV (1969-70), pp. 18-25) believes that the ditch is 'merely the moat round the castle.'

several stations ranging from Paradise to Hell seem to be grouped together in a line. Compare also the Fouquet miniature (though Southern says this shows part of an amphitheatre).[36]

The relative position of the stations is not indicated in the *Creacion*. Normally in England, Heaven seems to have been placed in the East (the position of the altar in a church), and Hell in the North, with the good characters in the South, and the worldly ones in the West; this is the positioning in the *Ordinalia*. Such an arrangement could still be retained in a semi-circle, with Heaven at centre back, Hell to the extreme left, and Paradise and the good characters to the right of Heaven. The World in the West would then be represented by the audience. On the other hand, the arrangement might have been more like that usual in the French plays, where Paradise and Heaven are placed on the left, and Hell on the extreme right,[37] as in both the Valenciennes and Fouquet miniatures. (This of course *is* Heaven's left).

One scene in the play seems to defy either of these arrangements of the *loca*, but there seems no possible organisation that would suit it. In Seth's account of his vision of Paradise, he describes the tree

36. Southern, pp. 91 ff. Schmitt (*op. cit.* pp.312-3), disagrees.
37. See Grace Frank, *The Medieval French Drama* (Oxford, 1954), p. 164.

whose branches reach up into Heaven, while its roots run down into Hell. If this vision were to be represented on stage, Paradise would need to be on a level between Heaven and Hell. This would involve an impossibly cumbersome structure, since both Heaven and Hell have more than one level. Probably the production did not attempt to stage this part of Seth's vision: he gives two detailed descriptions of Paradise; possibly because the audience was not shown all of the vision. The arrangement of the tree's roots and branches is not mentioned in the stage directions, although other elements of his vision, the Virgin in the Tree, and Cain in Hell, are detailed in the directions at 1772 and 1804.

There are other factors to take into account besides the evidence relating to the stations. In the directions to the actors, great emphasis is laid on the expression of emotion. While this can be done by the kind of physical movement that an audience could see from a distance, e.g.:

> *Eva is sorowfull, tereth her heare, and falleth downe upon Adam. He conforteth her* (1246 sd.)

and the direction to Cain to *look down and quake* quoted above, in the *Creacion* actors are frequently directed to convey feelings by facial expression:

> *Then Eva wondreth of the Serpent when she speaketh* (549 sd.)

Let Eva looke angerly on the Serpent and profer to departe (626 sd.)

Eva loketh upon Adam very stranglye (865 sd.)

Such emphasis on facial expression would tend to suggest a rather smaller type of theatre than at least the surviving Cornish rounds (St. Just is 126 ft. in diameter). The expressions and gestures the actors are directed to make in the *Creacion* are rather intimate, not of the grand kind essential to displaying oneself on a raised station:

hic pompabit Abraham (*OM* 1258 sd.)

filling a large area of the *place:*

Et verberabit eos super terram (*Castle*, 1777 sd.)

or making the most of both stations and place, as in the famous direction in the Coventry pageant:

Here Erode ragis in the pagond and in the street also (*Coventry*, p. 27, l. 783 sd.)

The speeches, too, are generally short, suggesting that the actors did not have a large area of *place* to cross while they were speaking.

I imagine, then, a much more intimate kind of setting for the production of the *Creacion* than that evidently used by the other Cornish plays, and, though it may be sacrilege to suggest it, there is no reason why this play should not have been performed inside, like some of the moral plays with which it has much in common.[38] The various effects, such as the puppets in

38. *Playne* could again be compared to *place*, which in Tudor Drama often means simply 'the hall floor'.

the war in Heaven (326 sd.), and the mechanical cloud with hinged sections in which God was lowered from Heaven (see note on 1 sd.) would have been much more manageable inside.

There have been two modern productions of the *Creacion*, both in Cornwall, at Piran Round in 1973 (in the round) and in Bodmin Church in 1977.[39]

39. For information on these productions see *The Creation of the World* trans. Donald Raw, Lodenek Press, Cornwall, 1978, pp. 135-41.

2. Playwright and auspices

a. Evidence

The colophon tells us that the *Creacion* was 'wryten' in 1611 by one William Jordan, of whom nothing more is known than that he may have come from the parish of Wendron, in the borough of Helston.[40] Since the manuscript is a fair copy, William Jordan was probably only the scribe (see Section 4a below).

The play provides no clues as to where it was put together and performed, and no external evidence has yet been discovered. Tubalcain mocks Noah for building the Ark 'in the middle of the country, away from the sea' (2299), which might possibly indicate that the play was not performed near the coast. This would considerably limit the number of possible places of performance, as Cornwall has such a high proportion of sea-coast. However, Tubalcain's remark would be funnier if the sea were nearby (and the question is found in some analogues, see note on 2297-99) so perhaps no assumptions can be based upon it. Jenner remarks: 'William Jordan may well have arranged his *Creation* for performance in Crasken Round or the Plan-an-Gwary at Ruan of St. Hillary under the auspices of the clergy of Meneage. But of this we know nothing.[41]

40. See Davies Gilbert, *Parochial History of the County of Cornwall* (London, 1870), III, p. 312.
41. Henry Jenner, 'The Cornish Drama', *Celtic Review*, III (July 1906-April 1907), p. 373.

b. Deductions

We can however glean more information about the sort of person who put the *Creacion* together, from the play itself. I have shown above that the compiler of the *Creacion* must have played the part of God the Father in a version of *Origo Mundi*. It would be likely that he went on playing the same part (he could not do any better) and it must be significant that 'The Father's' speeches in the *Creacion* are always emphasised by a pointing hand (see plate 3).

If we assume that the playwright played God, we can make sense of the hitherto puzzling two references to the 'conveyor' in the stage directions:

> *Adam and Eva aparlet in whytt lether in a place apoynted by the conveyour, and not to be sene tyll they be called, and then knell and ryse*
>
> (343 sd.)
>
> *Lett Adam laye downe and slepe wher Eva ys, and she by the conveyour must be taken from Adam is syde*
>
> (392 sd.)

The word has been interpreted in various ways, none of which seems satisfactory. It has been taken to mean a kind of prompter similar to the ordinary of Carew's account:

> the players conne not their parts without booke, but are prompted by one called the Ordinary, who followeth at their back with the booke in his hand, and telleth them softly what they must pronounce aloud.
>
> (p. 71)[42]

Chambers suggested the ordinary and the *conveyour* were one and the same,[43] but the direction at 343 indicates a more important role for the *conveyour* than just prompting, while that at 392 denotes a physical action. M.D. Anderson implies that she thinks of the *conveyor* as a 'stage creator'[44] but this tells us little more than the *Creacion* direction. Nance thought that the *conveyour* was a kind of secret passage-way that allowed actors to enter unseen (compare *OED* convey *v.* 6: 'to manage secretly'), and he believed that the 'Devil's Spoon', a hollowed-out area in Piran Round, was used for this purpose,[45] but the suggestion has since been made that the 'Devil's Spoon' was a cooking trench.[46] Nance's suggestion seems invalid anyway, for the second mention of the *conveyour* indicates an agent or instrument: *by* in 392 sd. cannot mean 'beside', or even 'via.'

42. William L. Tribby 'The Medieval Prompter: A Reinterpretation', *Theatre Survey*, V (1964), pp. 71-6, doubts the accuracy of this account, as do I.
43. Chambers, II, p. 140.
44. Anderson, pp. 142-3.
45. 'Plen an gwary', pp. 203-5.
46. See Treve Holman, 'Cornish Plays and Playing Places', *Theatre Notebook*, IV, pt. 3 (April-June 1950), pp. 52-4.

It is helpful to compare an entry in the York Civic Records for 1486 which states that one Henry Hudson was appointed to have the '*conueance* of the making and directing of the shew' (a reception for Henry VII).[47] This means in effect the 'running' of the show (*OED* conveyance *sb.* 10: 'management'). Running a production of a miracle play, being a Pageant Master, meant, among other things, looking after the book of the play, possibly writing or redacting it.[48] A 'conveyor' may very well mean a redactor as well as a director/stage-manager (*OED* convey *v* 9b: 'to transmit to prosperity, to hand down'; 9d: 'to communicate; to express in words'; 12: 'to conduct (an affair); to carry on, manager'). In the direction at 343, *a place apoynted by the conveyour* obviously (in the light of the entry in the York Civic Records) means 'a place decided by the director/stage-manager'. However at 392 the *conveyour* seems (as Anderson implies) to mean God, for he says 'I will make a mate for you' just as the direction occurs. He has just taken a bone from *Adam is syde* (389 sd.) and in the iconography of this episode, of which there is a version in the Creation window at St. Neot (see plate 2, panel 5) God is shown lifting Eve from Adam. In 392 sd., then, *by the*

47. Sydney Anglo, *Spectacle, Pageantry, and Early Tudor Policy* (Oxford, 1969), p. 23 (my italics).
48. See Wickham, pp. 297-300.

conveyour ought to mean 'by God'; in fact it means 'by the redactor [who is playing God]'.

So in the *Creacion* the *conveyour* means the person who (1) 'wrote' (i.e. redacted) the *Creacion*; (2) stage-managed it (this explains why the manuscript contains both authorial instructions to the actors and entries we might expect from a prompt-book), and (3) played the part of God the Father in it. We may compare him with Robert Croo of Coventry who

> not only redacted the surviving *Shearman and Taylors'* Pageant and *Weavers'* Pageant and provided the Drapers with 'the boke' for their pageant, but wrote a play called *The Golden Fleece* for the Cappers. In addition he played the part of God in the Drapers Pageant of Doomsday in 1560, the book of which he provided three years earlier. That same year he was also paid 'for mendyng the devills cottes'. Four years earlier he had been paid 'for makyng iij worldys' and two years later 'for a hat for the pharysye'. There was thus hardly any aspect of the production with which he and his like were not familiar.[49]

The 'conveyor' of the *Creacion* is thus another example of the English pageant master Wickham describes. He must have been a Cornishman whose first language was English, since the play has an English title and stage-directions. He put on a production of the play some time before 1611 (probably in the sixteenth century, see below), having prepared a text of the play at least partly from memory, which he then used as a prompt-book, writing notes on it as he gave his directions to the actors. In 1611 William Jordan

49. Wickham, p. 299.

(who was almost certainly *not* the 'conveyor', since he was apparently incapable of distinguishing between different types of stage direction) made a fair copy of this prompt book, probably to preserve the play for posterity, perhaps intending to start a commonplace book, or collection of similar pieces in Cornish.

3. Date

There is no problem about the date of the *manuscript*, since we are told that this was 'wryten in 1611', and this date accords with the handwriting and binding. But the manuscript is William Jordan's fair copy of a producer's prompt-book (see above), so that it is the date of this prompt-book, when the play was put on in its present form, that we need to try to establish. There are several aspects of the *Creacion* that may be considered in an attempt to arrive at a possible date, but none of them serves as any very useful guide.

i. The Cornish Language. If more were known about the history of the Cornish language, especially in its later stages, a study of the state of the language in the *Creacion* might help towards suggesting a date for the play. But no authoritative history of the language has yet been written, and besides, the problem is a circular one: as the *Creacion* is one of the few surviving examples of written Cornish, a knowledge of the play's date is an important prerequisite to writing a history of Cornish. However, the *Creacion* is likely to be at least a century later than the *Ordinalia*, because of changes in spelling, and because the former has a much higher proportion of 'English' words. For example, where *Origo Mundi* has 'Adam saf yn ban yn clor/Ha treyl the gyk ha the woys' (65-6),

Creacion reads 'Adam save in ban in *cloer*/Ha trayle ʒa gyke ha tha *owg*,' showing the diphthongisation of *o* to *oe*; the voicing of *th* to ʒ; and the softening of *s* to *g*;[50] and compare 'Ythyn in nef ha bestas' (*OM* 118), and 'Ha tolle the bryes len' (*OM* 294), with 'Ethen in *ayre*, ha bestas' (*Creacion*, 399), and 'Ha tulla tha bryas *leell*' (*Creacion*, 892), where the Cornish word is replaced by an 'English' one. Elements in the *Creacion* such as these are features of later Cornish, but as there is no adequate survey of the language to use as a guide, they cannot give any precise indication as to date. Some of the spelling variations may be topographical, and the question of the inclusion of 'English' words is particularly problematical, as we have no knowledge of when or how such words entered the Cornish language: whether through English, or directly from French or Latin. Many of the 'English' words in the *Creacion* are latinate, especially the infinitives and past participles (*accomptys, acquyttya, affynes, amendya, appoyntys, assaya, assentys, attendya, avysshes*, etc.). These probably entered the language later than words like *honor* and *vertewe*, and there are many more of them than in the *Ordinalia*. Fuller knowledge about questions such as these would help to

50. Lists of such spelling and sound changes may be found in Lhuyd, p. 231, and Stokes, pp. 3-4. Two points may be added: that initial mutation occurs much less regularly in *Creacion*; and that separation of the adverbial prefix is common.

date the play more accurately. However, we can say that the language and spelling cannot possibly be earlier than 1500, and probably later: the spelling *dn* for *nn* never appears before c. 1560.[51] Nance dated the play 'about 1530' on the basis of the language.[52]

ii. The English Language. *Creacion* contains English stage directions, and also some phrases and sentences that occur in the dialogue, mostly in the speeches of Lucifer and the bad characters (see note on 113). These are unaffected by the Cornish, that is they are noticeably 'foreign' snatches of English, rather than naturalisations into Cornish as are the 'English' words discussed above. Stokes felt that the occurrence of forms like *every chone* seem to suggest a date prior to 1611 (p. 4) - examples he does not mention are the pronouns *hem* and *hes*, which do not normally appear after 1500. But the English spoken and written in Cornwall obviously has dialectical variants, and we can draw no definite conclusions here.

iii. The Subject Matter. There are some elements in the play that might provide some indication as to

51. Except for one example in *Meriasek* (which may itself be later?). I am grateful to Oliver Padel for this information, as for so much else on Cornish and other Celtic languages.
52. Nance, p. [1].

date: i.e. the references to Roman Catholic doctrine. The play lays a strong stress on the difference between Hell and Limbo, especially in Lucifer's speech 2020 ff. There are different *mansyons* in Hell (2021). The Virgin Mary is incorporated, apparently uniquely, into the legend of Seth's vision of the Tree of Life (see note on 1802 ff.), while incense is used by Abel and Noah. These elements may suggest that the *Creacion* was put together in its present form before the Reformation: they might otherwise have been deleted, as were for example references to the Sacraments and Transubstantiation in the Towneley plays.[53] However, they might equally well have survived from an earlier version, or, since Devon and Cornwall resisted the Reformation much longer than the rest of England,[54] these elements might actually have been included deliberately. Thus such material cannot really provide evidence of a pre-Reformation date, as Stokes thought,[55] in fact the defiant emphasis on Marian doctrine may indicate the opposite. The presence of Mary in the Tree of Life, for instance, has been *added* by the playwright to the legend, possibly in *reaction* to the Reformation.

53. Gardiner, *op. cit.*, p. 61. He also notes that plays concerning the Virgin Mary were excised from the York cycle.
54. See A.S.D. Smith, *The Story of the Cornish Language* (Camborne, 1947), p. 8; Jenner, p. 12.
55. See Stokes, p. 4.

On the whole, then, we can say that the *Creacion* was put together certainly later than 1500, perhaps in the 1550's, when Catholicism was back in the reign of Queen Mary, or possibly even later. We have Carew's evidence that plays resembling miracle plays were still being presented in Cornwall as late as 1602: the *Creacion* could perhaps have been put together for actual performance even as late as this. Obviously this does not mean that the entire play was newly composed at this late date; the evidence of its relationship with *Origo Mundi* shows that at least part of the play was based on a version known from oral tradition, and the compiler may well have been basing all of the play on words that had been in use for a long time in productions of Cornish miracle plays (this would explain the existence of elements in the subject-matter that seem anachronistic). In 1611 William Jordan copied the play, probably to make a record of it, feeling that the miracle plays would soon cease to be performed. He may also have wished to preserve an example of the fast-disappearing Cornish language. Carew also records that 'most of the Inhabitants [of Cornwall] can no word of *Cornish*', (p. 56), and although this may be an exaggeration, knowledge of Cornish certainly belonged only to a priviledged few by 1698, when Keigwyn made his translations of the surviving plays.

4. Text

a. Manuscript and previous editions

The *Creacion* exists in a unique manuscript, Bodleian MS. 219. This is a paper manuscript of 95 folios, 12½ by 3¾ inches, numbered i-xxiv, 1-74. The binding is limp white parchment with gold ornamentation, and has the initials J.K. (?John Keigwyn). Folios iii-xxiv, 28-74 are blank; f. i contains the Bodleian MS number, while on f. ii, a later paper, lines 2083-93 are copied out in a later hand. Ff. 1-27 contain the text of *The Creacion of the World*, written in a secretary hand. The colophon states that the manuscript was written by William Jordan in 1611, a date that accords with the handwriting and binding. The provenance of the manuscript is not known; it was probably acquired by the Bodleian library in 1611-15.[56]

The manuscript is a fair copy, and it is possible to discern at least three stages of its written development:

i. The text was written out (or dictated to a scribe) by someone who had reconstructed at least part of it from memory (see Section 1c above). At this stage, probably, directions to the actors, and on the design of the sets, were inserted. These usually begin with the

56. *A Summary catalogue of Western Manuscripts in the Bodleian Library at Oxford*, ed. F. Madan and H.H. Craster (Oxford, 1922), II, i, 568.

formula 'Let x do so and so' or 'Let x be done' and are often quite lengthy and detailed.

ii. This copy was then used by the stage-manager as a prompt-book. He added notes about the actors' movements, and on the props that had to be ready. These can be clearly distinguished from the directions written in stage (i). They are usually brief (*a chawbone readye*) and generally occur several lines earlier in the manuscript than the scene in which they are needed. (This is what mainly makes it clear that they were added at a later stage. See especially note on 1772 sd.). I give my reasons above (Section 2b) for assuming that the 'writers' in both i and ii are the same person, i.e. the 'conveyor'.

iii. A fair copy (the present MS) was made of this prompt-book, probably not by the same person because he makes no attempt to distinguish the two types of stage direction, copying them all out neatly in the right-hand margin of the MS.

This was very probably intended to be the first item in a commonplace book, but nothing further was ever written in it.

A transcription and translation of this manuscript was made in 1691 for Jonathan Trelawney, Bishop of Exeter, by John Keigwyn of Mousehole, in Cornwall. Several copies of this survive, including what is probably the original:

i. Bodleian MS. Corn. e. 2. This is dated 1691, and is probably in Keigwyn's autograph. It was revised by Thomas Tonkin, the Cornish antiquarian, and William Hals, the Cornish historian. It was presented to the Bodleian by Edwin Ley, whose father inherited it from Tonkin.[57]

ii. British Library MS. Harl. 1867. This manuscript also contains some of Edward Lhuyd's letters, and a collection of Welsh proverbs. The copy is written in several hands, and has corrections made by Lhuyd, who collated it with Bodleian MS. 219 in 1702. It was presented to the British Library by the Rev. Moses Williams.[58]

iii. A copy transcribed by John Moore in 1698, in the Gatley Collection bequeathed to the Museum of the Royal Institution of Cornwall in 1885, by George Freeth of Duporth. This copy had belonged to W.C. Borlase, but nothing is known of its whereabouts in the early nineteenth century.[59]

iv. A copy also containing Keigwyn's version of the Cornish passion poem, originally in the

57. *Ibid.*, V, 475-6.
58. *A Catalogue of the Harleian Manuscripts in the British Museum* (London 1808), II, 272.
59. This copy must be identical with that entered in Boase and Courtney, II, 1250, as 'by J. Meney? penes W.C. Borlase'.

collection of Davies Gilbert, and used by him in his edition of the play. This copy was sold at Sotheby's on 22nd March, 1917, to a certain 'Potter'.

This list differs somewhat from that given by Stokes and followed by Chambers and Stratman, as they did not know of copies iii and iv. The copy they list as being in the possession of J.C. Hotten the bookseller is not a manuscript, but a printed copy of Davies Gilbert's edition.[60] A further copy stated to be in Lord Bute's library[61] is of Keigwyn's version of the *Ordinalia*, not the *Creacion*.

There are also copies of parts of Keigwyn's version of the play in various eighteenth-century commonplace books, the longest being in that of William Gwavas, British Library Add. MS. 28, 554, pages 24-49 of which contain *Creacion* 1803-end, and there is a copy of this in the Museum of the Royal Institution of Cornwall.

All these copies derive from Bodleian MS. 219, from which Keigwyn made his original transcription, so that none of them can have any independent textual authority, but their translations, though often extremely inaccurate, are sometimes of value.

60. See John Camden Hotten, *A Handbook to the Topography and Family History of England and Wales* (London, 1863), p. 28.
61. See Boase and Courtney, III, p. 1250.

The *Creacion* was first published in a version by Davies Gilbert,[62] in Keigwyn's translation. The first genuine edition is that of Stokes, published in 1863, which contains his own transcription and translation of the original manuscript. Nance produced a lithograph version of the play in Unified Cornish with a new translation, in 1959. The present edition is greatly indebted to the work of both Stokes and Nance.

b. <u>This edition</u>

This edition will appear more conservative than those of Stokes and Nance, for they often emended what they took to be irregularities in spelling or syntax. My practice has been to retain the reading of the manuscript wherever possible, for although the play often has a word (or form of a word) that is not recorded elsewhere, so little Cornish survives, especially of this period, that one cannot say with any certainty that such words are not genuine. Instances of curious word division, and n/m variation (where a linguist would probably wish to emend) may reflect the habits of the scribe, which are themselves of interest.

Where an emendation has been made, the manuscript

62. *The Creation of the World, with Noah's Flood: written in Cornish in the year 1611, by William Jordan: with an English Translation by John Keigwyn* (London, 1827). This is merely a printed version of Keigwyn.

reading is collated, with those of Stokes and Nance when they are significant. (Nance) indicates that he is responsible for an emendation but has used different (i.e. Unified) spelling. I have not cited every instance where my reading differs from that of Stokes because his edition contains a very large number of printing errors. Every difference between readings has been re-checked against the manuscript. I have appended a table collating Stokes's line-numbering with my own, for ease of reference and comparison. (See Appendix IV.)

Abbreviations have been silently expanded except in cases of doubt or difference of opinion about what the expansion should be, when the manuscript reading has been collated. Roman numerals have been changed to the appropriate Cornish (or English in the speech-headings). Punctuation, including capitalisation, conforms to modern usage. This is meant as an aid to reading; if the verse were spoken it would provide its own punctuation. The word division and spelling of the manuscript have been retained, except that consonantal i and u are normalised to j and v. Stage-directions, which are mainly written in the right-hand margin of the manuscript (see Plate 3), have been placed next to the line to which they appear to refer, although they sometimes occur earlier in the manuscript for the convenience of the stage-manager, or occupy a whole stanza's space. A few directions have been added to help the reader visualise the action:

these appear in square brackets.

The translation is not meant to be a line by line gloss like that of Stokes, aimed at specialists in the Cornish language who are interested in the finer points of Cornish syntax and vocabulary. It is intended to be a readable, and perhaps even actable version, primarily for those interested in the early drama, but also for the general reader. If it were intended primarily as an acting version the translation would have been much freer: as it is I have tried to stay as close to the meaning of the middle Cornish verse as is consistent with modern English prose. Originally I made no attempt to follow the arrangement of the Cornish lines, but it has seemed better to do this for purposes of reference. I must emphasise, however, that my version is supposed to be read as prose, not as cock-up verse. I have occasionally had to reverse the order of the Cornish lines in order to produce a sensible English sentence, and have sometimes had to move a verb from its 'proper' place in one verse line to another in the translation. Also I have not always stuck rigidly to the Cornish syntax: this is especially so in clauses of result where it has sometimes sounded more natural to render *may*, 'so that', as 'and' (e.g. 1253, 1267). Impersonal constructions such as *marth ew genaf*, lit. 'amazement is with me' only sound right as personal ones in English, i.e. 'I am amazed'. Relative clauses with *es* 'who is' have usually been turned into phrases with *es* omitted (e.g. 549, 1962), and similar treatment has been given to the relative *henna* 'that' when it anticipates an object (e.g. 121-2, 126-7). Cornish often uses collective plurals where we would have a singular: *frutes, paynes, dorrowe* 'waters'. In these cases plural is only kept for a special reason (such as *Effarnowe* lit. 'Hells', see note on 2020 ff). The ethic dative has no modern equivalent, though I have tried to take it into account. The second person singular has not been translated as 'thou' but as 'you'. It might have been retained for God, but it seemed best to be consistent. The greatest difficulty has been in the translation of expletives and insults, since many of the expressions used in the *Creacion* do not have any modern equivalent. We do not now call a man *horssen kam* (lit. 'crooked whoreson'): somehow 'twisted son-of-a-bitch' does not sound right. I have mulled over many alternatives, and if the reader is displeased with my solutions, then I urge him to try for himself.

The greatest difference of opinion among those from whom I have taken advice about this book has been over the translation, and the style I have chosen after much thought will doubtless not suit everybody. To convey the feeling of the original really closely I would have had to use sixteenth-century English. But I have tried not to add any flavour, and to be as plain as possible.

2. *The Creation Window*, St. Neot Church, Cornwall.

The
Creacion of the World

The First Daie of Playe

The Father in Heaven

(The Father must be in a clowde, and when he speakethe of Heaven, let the levys open). 1r

Ego sum Alpha et Omega:
Heb dallathe na dowethva
Pur wyre me ew.

Omma agy than clowdes,
War face an dower in sertan,
Try person in idn dewges
Ow kys raynya bys vickan
Yn mere honor ha vertewe.

Me hawe Mabe han Spirisans
Try ython in un substance,
Comprehendys in udn Dew.

Me ew henwis Dew an Tase,
Ol gollosacke dres pub tra.
Skon y fythe gwrys der ow rase
Neve, place ryall thom trigva,
Hawe thron setha owe bothe ewe
May fo henna.

Han noore in wethe a wollas
Scon worthe compas avyth gwryes.
Honna a vythe ow skavall droose
Rag ow pleasure pub preyse,
Ha thom honor maga ta.

4. agy than (*Nance*); avythan *MS;* avy than *Stokes.*
12. *Marginal note* Genesis capite primo

The Father in Heaven

(The Father must be in a cloud, and when he speaks of Heaven, let the leaves open)

Ego sum Alpha et Omega:
Without beginning nor end
very truly I am.

Here within the clouds,
upon the face of the water indeed;
three persons in one godhead
reigning together eternally
in great honour and power.

I and my son and the Holy Spirit
we are three in one substance,
comprehended in one God.

I am named God the Father,
almighty above everything.
At once shall be made through my grace
Heaven, a splendid place for my dwelling,
and my will is that that
be the seat of my throne.

And also the earth below
shall at once be made in due proportion.
That shall be my footstool
for my pleasure at all times,
and to my honour also.

Neve omma ew gwryes genaf,
Orthe ow devyes in serten.
Hag yny y fythe gorrys
Neb an gorth gans joye ha cane.
Naw order elath gloryes
Y a vythe, ryall ha splan,
Canhasawe them danvenys
Rage ow servia bys vickan
Me avyn may fons nevra.

Lemyn pub order thy seat
Me a vyn may fo gorrys,
Ha pub onyn thy thecree
A vyth gorrys ʒom service
Pan vidnaf ve comanndya.

Omma nessa thom throne ve
An kensa try a vithe gwryes:
Cherubyn, an ughella
Ty a vyth, des arage uskys
Seraphyn, inwethe Tronys.

Owe gwerthya oll why a wra,
Pare dellywe owe bothe nefra,
Omma pub pryes.

Ha te, Lucyfer golowe,
Yn della ew tha hanowe.
Ughe pub eall ty a ysa.

An kensa order ty ywe. 1v
Gwayte ow gworria war bub tewe,
Ʒeso gy pardel gotha.

Heaven here is made by me [*Heaven revealed*],
according to my plan indeed.
And in it shall be put
those who will worship me with joyful song.
Nine orders of glorious angels
they shall be, splendid and bright:
I will that they ever be
messengers for me, sent
to serve me eternally.

Now I will that every order
be set on its throne,
and every one in its degree
shall be put to my service
when I shall command.

Here next to my throne
the first three shall be made:
Cherubin, you shall be the highest;
come forth quickly
Seraphin; Thrones too.

You shall all worship me,
as it is my will always,
here at all times.

And you, bright Lucifer
(such is your name),
you shall sit above every angel.

You are the first order.
Take care to worship me everywhere,
as it behoves you.

In second degre yfithe gwryes
Try order moy, yn sertan:
Des arage thym, Pryncipatys;
Tee a seathe oma poran,
    Potestas inbarth arall.

Domynashon yn tewma,
Ow praysya hag ow laudia
    Ow hanow nefra heb gyll.

An tryssa degre a wolas
Me a wra try order moy:
Arthelath, order pur vras,
Dewgh a rag omma ʒa vee,
    Ha Vertutis kekeffrys.

Han Elath, yn barth dyhow
Why a seath omma heb gowe.
Them y fethow canhagowe,
Hag y wrewgh ow aradowe
    Gans joy bras ha cane pub preyse.

Lebmyn pan ew thymo gwryes
Neve ha noore orth both ow bryes,
Han naw order collenwys
Han kynsa jorna spedyes,
    My asone gans owe ganowe,

Hag a vyn diskynnya
Than noore in dan an clowdys,
Hag ow both gwethill ena
Me a vyn, may fo gwellys
    Ow bosaf Dew heb parow.

58. Ow hanow *Nance:* tha hanow *MS.*

In the second degree shall be made
three further orders, indeed:
come forward to me, Principalities;
you shall sit right here,
Power on the other hand.

Domination on this side
praising and honouring
my name eternally, in truth.

Of the third degree below
I will create three further orders:
Archangels, a very great order,
come forward here to me,
and Virtues too.

And the Angels, on the right hand
here you shall sit, truly.
You shall be messengers for me,
and do my commands
with great joy and song always.

Now since for me is made
Heaven and earth according to my mind's wish
and the nine orders completed
and the first day done,
I will bless them with my mouth.

And I will descend
to the earth beneath the clouds,
and I shall do my will there,
that it may be seen
that I am God unparalleled.

[*God descends to earth.*]

Lebmyn yn second jorna
Gwraf broster a thesempys:
Yn yborn es a wartha
Me a vyn bos golow gwryes.

Hag yn weth bos deberthva
Sure inter an gyth han noos.
Ny fyll thym cudnyke a dra
War an byes der ow gallus.

An moar brase yn cutt termyn
A dro thom tyre a vyth dreys,
Rag y wetha pur elyn
Orth harlutry prest pub preys.

An tryssa dyth me a wra 2r
Than gwyth sevall yn ban,
Ha doen dellyow teke ha da
Ha flowres wheag, in serten.

Ow blonogath yw henna,
May tockans unna pur splan
Frutes thom both, rag maga
Seyl a theyg bewnans hogan.

In peswera dyth bith gwryes
An howle han loer in tevery,
Han steare in weth kekeffrys,
Rag gwyle golow venary.
An ryma yw fyne gonethys;
Ow bannath y rof thethy.

Now on the second day
I will at once make splendour:
I will that light be made
in the sky that is above.

And also that there be a division
surely between the day and the night.
I shall not lack knowledge of anything
on the earth through my power.

In a short time the great sea
shall be brought about my land,
in order to keep it very pure
from pollution ever at all times.

The third day I will make
the trees stand up,
and bear good and beautiful leaves
and sweet flowers, in truth.

That is my will,
that they may bring forth upon them abundantly
fruit to my liking, in order to feed
those who shall live hereafter.

On the fourth day shall be made
the sun and the moon also,
and the stars as well too,
to make light always.
These are well made;
I give my blessing to them.

In pympas dyth, orth ow breis,
An puskas, heb falladowe,
Hag oll an ethyn keffrys,
Me as gwra thom plegadow,
Hag oll an bestas yn beyse,
Gans prevas a bub sortowe.
An ryma ew oll teke gwryes:
Me as sone war barth, heb gowe.

Lucyfer in Heaven

Pays, I say, oll elath Nef!
Golsowowh tha ve lemyn!
Cresowh ow bosaf prince creif,
Hag in weth thewhy cheften
    Bean ha brase.

Lucyfer ew ow hanowe,
Pensevicke in Nef omma.
Ow howetha ew tanow;
Why a wore ynta henna:
    Ow bosaf gwell es an Tase.

Me ew lantorn Nef, ywys,
Avell tane ow collowye,
Moy splanna es an Drengys.
Henna degowhe destynye,
    Om bosof prynce pur gloryous.

Oll gans ower ow terlentry
Y thesaf, heb dowte in case;
Splanna es an howle deverye,
Why a yll warbarthe gwelas
    Ow bosaf, sertayn pub preyse.

108. plegadow *Stokes;* falladow *MS.*

On the fifth day, according to my will,
I will make the fish, without fail,
and all the birds too,
for my pleasure,
and all the animals in the world,
with reptiles of all kinds.
These are all beautifully made:
I will bless them all together, indeed.

Lucifer in Heaven

Quiet, I say, all angels of Heaven!
Now listen to me!
Believe that I'm a mighty prince
and also leader to you
small and great.

Lucifer is my name,
a prince here in Heaven.
Few are my equals;
you know well
that I am better than the Father.

I am the lamp of Heaven, in truth,
shining like fire,
more splendid than the Trinity.
Bear witness to
my being a most glorious prince.

All shining with gold
I am, without doubt in the matter;
you can all see together
that I am more splendid indeed than the sun,
surely at all times.

Ny vannaf orth eale na moy 2v
Dos thom statma menas me;
Henna ew ow thowle, devery.

Maga vras ove avell Dew;
Me a gommand war bub tew
Myns es yn Neif thom gworthya.

Elathe oll, why a glowas,
Pandra gowsow thym lemyn?
Delnagoma polat brase?
Gorrybowhe oll pub onyn,
Why a wore pythoma.

An Tase gallas a lemma.
Me a dowle ny the omma
Bys vyckan mar a callaf.

Angell of Lucyfer

Lucyfer, te ew henna
Sure a bashe myns es in Nef.
Creatys nobell omma
Y thota, nature creif,
Ha mean creys.

Sure rag henna
Theth honora
Me avyn, uhan Drenges.

Angell of God in that degre

Te creature unkunda,
Warbyn ȝa vaker ow cowse!
Predery prage na wreta
Y festa gwryes, te gwase lowse,
Gans Dew omma?

Gansa pan wres comparya
Mer tha vlamya y thosta
Ha paynes yfyth ragtho.

I don't want any other angel
to come to my state except myself;
that is my will, indeed.

I am as great as God;
I command everywhere
all that are in Heaven to worship me.

You have heard, angels all,
what do you say to me now?
So aren't I a fine fellow?
All answer, every one,
you know what I am.

The Father has gone from here.
I mean him not to come here
ever again, if I can.

Angel of Lucifer

Lucifer, you are that
indeed that surpasses all in Heaven.
Created noble here
you are, strong in nature,
and I believe it.

So certainly
honour you
above the Trinity will I.

Angel of God in that degree

You unnatural creature,
speaking against your maker!
Why do you not consider
that you were made, you nasty piece of work,
here by God?

When you vie with him
you are greatly to blame
and there will be punishment for it.

Angell of Lucyfer in the second degre speaketh knelinge

Pyw henna a veth mar vold
Cowse gear warbyn Lucyfer?
Heare he hath unto you told
That in Heven ys not his peare,
    Ha mean creyse.

Why an gweall ow terlentry
Splanna es an howle devery.
    Me ath honor them dell reyse.

Angell of God in that degre

A taw, nagowse a henna
Me ath pys; creys ow lavar:
Neb an formyas ev omma
An deform arta, predar,
    Y voth panvo.

Mar tregowhe in gregyans na
Morath why as byth ragtha,
    Trustyowh ȝotha.

Angell of Lucyfer in the third degre speketh kneling

Pennagel ew na lavara
Nagew Lucyfer worthy
Omma thagan governa
Ha bos pedn in Nef defry,
    A lavar gowe.

Yea, ha worthy pub preyse 3r
Tha vos yn trone ysethys
    Avel Dew, sure heb parawe.

Mean gorth omma del ryes,
War ow dew glyen kekeffrys,
    Rag y bos mar garadow.

171-2. a henna/Me ath pys; creys *this ed;* a henna,/my a'th pys crys *Nance.*
179 sp. *kneling* knelng *MS.*

Angel of Lucifer in the second degree speaks kneeling

Who is that who is so bold
to speak a word against Lucifer?
Here he has told you
that in Heaven is not his peer,
and I believe it.

You see him shining
more splendid indeed than the sun.
[*To Lucifer*] I will honour you as I ought.

Angel of God in that degree

Ah quiet, do not speak of that
I beg you; take my word:
He who formed him here
will deform him again, remember,
when it is his will.

If you persist in that belief
you will regret it,
be sure of that.

Angel of Lucifer in the third degree speaks kneeling

Whoever it is that denies
that Lucifer is worthy
to govern us here
and indeed to be head in Heaven,
tells a lie.

Yes, and worthy always
to be seated on a throne
like God, indeed unequalled.

I will worship him here as is need,
on my knees too,
because he is so worthy of love.

Lucyfer in Heaven

Dell wrama raynya omma
Yn trone wartha gans glorye,
Why a sethe warbarth genaf,
Myns a golha ortha vee,
    Poran ryb ow thenewan.

I was made of a thought:
Ye may be glad of suche wight.
And in Heaven so gay I-wrought
Semely am in every sight.
    Com up to me, every chone.

Hag in urna
Gwraf assaya
    ȝa vos mester war an trone.

Let hem offer to assend to the trone. The Angell stayethe hem.

Angell of God in the third degre

Te, Lucifer, unkunda
Meer ythos ortha vaker.
Dowt ythew theis rag henna
Gawas meare y displeasure,
    Del os worthy ȝa henna.

Praga na wreta predery
Y festa formys, devery,
    Der y wreans eve omma?

Der henna, predar inta,
Ef a yll der geare arta
    Theth destrowhy, skemynys.

202. mester *Nance;* $\overset{3}{\text{m}}$ *MS:* mur *Stokes.*
202 sd. *after 194 in MS.*
203 sp. *Angell (Nance);* 3 Angell *MS.*

Lucifer in Heaven

As I do reign here
with glory on a throne above,
you shall sit together with me,
all who listen to me,
right by my side.

I was made in a trice:
you may be glad of such a creature.
And in Heaven made so bright
I am attractive in the sight of all.
Come up to me, everyone.

And then
I shall try
to be master on the throne.

Let him attempt to ascend to the throne. The Angel stays him.

Angel of God in the third degree

Lucifer, you are most unnatural
towards your maker.
Therefore you are in danger
of earning his great displeasure,
as you are worthy of that.

Why do you not consider
that you were formed, in truth,
here through his creation?

From that, consider well,
He can again by a word
destroy you, cursed one.

Lucifer in Heaven

Ty, Myhall, re stowte ythos
Pan wres ortha vy settya.
Me agrys hagan suppose
Y fynses sche comparya
Lemyn genaf.

Na wres, na wres, nabarth dowte,
Ty, na oll tha gowetha;
Mar qwreth me ages clowte.
Rag henna gwrewh owe gorthya
Ha warbarth trustyowh unnaf.

Why am gweell ow terlentry
Splanna es an Tas deffry;
Henna cresowhe om bosaf.

The Father

(The Father commethe before Heven and speaketh to Lucyfer) A Lucyfer, Lucyfer,
Te a ve oll lantorn Nef,
Ha drethaf serten pub eare
Te a ve exaltys breyf,
Hag ath settyas pur ughall.

Lemyn mere os unkunda 3v
Orthaf vy panwres settya.
Rag ʒa oth tha bayne nefra
Ty awra dyiskynya
Mahellas ysall.

Determys ove ʒa undra,
Ha concludys magata;
Tha wythyll un dean omma
A thore ha sleme ʒom servia,
Hath place she tha opea,

227 sp. *this ed;* The father in heaven *MS.*

Lucifer in Heaven

Michael, *you* are too bold
when you oppose *me*.
I believe and suppose
you would vie
with me now.

You shall not, you shall not, have no fear,
you nor all your comrades;
if you do I shall clout you.
Therefore worship me
and together trust in me.

You see me shining
more splendid indeed than the Father;
that believe that I am.

The Father

(The Father comes in front of Heaven and speaks to Lucifer) Ah, Lucifer, Lucifer,
you *were* all the light of Heaven,
and certainly always by me
you were greatly exalted,
and set yourself very high.

Now you are greatly unnatural
when you set yourself against me.
For your pride to pain eternally
you will descend
that you may go below.

I have determined on one thing,
and decided too:
to make a man here
from earth and slime to serve me,
and to make available your place:

Rage collenwall an romes
A vyth voyd yn Nef uskys
Drethas sche hath cowetha.

Lett Hell gape when the Father nameth yt.

Efarn ragas a vyth gwrys:
Uskys commandyaf henna.
Ena ty a vyth tregys,
Ha myns assentyas genas
    Genas sche an naw order.

In paynes bys venary
Heb rawnson vetholl na fyne,
Yna pub eare ow murnya
Rag gallarowe, bys worffen,
    Why a vith, me a levar.

Lucyfer in Heaven

Ay! A vynta ge orth mab dean
Pan vo gwryes a slem hager
Occupya rage sertayne
Ow rome ve, nagevas peare
    Omma in Neve?

Henna vea hager dra!
Den a vynta gule a bry
ʒa thos omma then plasma
Neb ew lenwys a glorye?
    Ragtha worthy nynjew ef!

Na, na, ny vythe in della,
Me a worthib theis henna.
An place sure lowre ʒa warta
Me a wyth whath, rom lowta,
    Ha tha worthys sche keffrys.

to fill the spaces
that will at once be empty in Heaven
through you and your associates.

Let Hell gape when the Father names it.
Hell shall be made for you:
I command that at once.
There you shall stay,
and all of the nine orders
who took your part with you.

In everlasting pain
without any ransom or limit,
wailing there always
for sorrow until the end
you shall be, I say.

Lucifer in Heaven

What! Do you want mankind
when he is made of foul slime
to occupy for certain
my place, who have no peer
here in Heaven?

That would be a foul thing!
Would you make a man of clay
come here to this place
which is full of glory?
He is not worthy of it!

No, no, it will not be so,
I answer you that.
I shall keep the place sure enough from him
yet, by my faith,
and from you as well.

Ty am gweall ve creif omma
Whath pur browt ow trebytchya.
Hanter an elath genaffa
Assentyes ythyns, sera,
Thom mayntaynya in spyte thys,
Dell welta ge.

For well nor wo
I will not go.
I saye yowe so.
This will not be,
Thymo ve creis.

Rag me a umsens
Serten ugh pub myns
A ve bythqwath whath formys.

The Father Taw, Lucyfer melegas, 4r
In gollan del os gothys.
Rag skon ty a tha baynes
Heb redempcyon, thyma creys,
Sure thymo creys.

Oll tha splandar hath tectar
Y trayle skon theis tha hacter,
Ha mere utheck byllan.

Myghale, pryns ow chyvalry,
Han elath an order nawe,
An rebellyans ma deffry -
Than doer ganso, mester ha mawe,
Tha Efarn, hager trygva.

Ena tregans yn paynes,
Ha golarowe mere pub pryes,
Yn pur serten rag nefra.

295. mester *Nance;* $\overset{3}{m}$ *MS;* mergh *Stokes.*

You will see me strong here
falling still very proudly.
Half the angels
are in agreement with me, sir,
to support me in spite of you,
as you shall see.

For joy or woe
I will not go.
I tell you so.
This will not be,
believe me.

For I consider myself
certainly above all
that have ever yet been created.

The Father

Quiet, cursed Lucifer,
proud in heart as you are.
For at once you shall go to punishment
without redemption, believe me,
believe me indeed.

All your brightness and your beauty
shall turn at once to horror for you,
and very frightful deviltry.

Michael, chief of my army,
and angels of the nine orders,
this rebellience indeed -
down with them, master and man,
to Hell, an ugly home.

There let them stay in pains,
and great sorrows always,
surely for ever.

All Angells must have swordys and staves, and must com to the rome wher Lucyfer ys.

Mychaell
Dewne warbarth, an nawe order!
Hellyn yn mes Lucyfer
    Athesempys mes an Nef.

Lucyfer
Ty, chet, gwraf tha examnya:
Prage y fyn Dew ow damnya,
    Ha me mar gollowe ha creif?

Mychaell
Rag y bosta melagas
Hag in golan re othys:
    Der reson thys me a breif.

Ty foole, prag na bredersys
A thorn Dew y festa gwryes,
Yn weth ganso exaltys
Dres myns eall in Nef sethys
    Oma ydn y drone sethys?

Lucyfer
Even in trone manaf setha,
    (Let Lucyfer offer to go upe to the trone)
Han keth place mannaf gwetha
    Whath, in spyta theis.

Keffrys me ham cowetha
Der gletha a vyn trea
Owe bosaf moy worthy
    Agys an Tase, sure pub pryes.

All Angels must have swords and staves, and must come to the place where Lucifer is.

Michael

Let us come together, the nine orders!
Let us drive out Lucifer
immediately from Heaven.

Lucifer

You, fellow, I will question you:
why will God damn me,
and I so bright and strong?

Michael

Because you are cursed
and too proud in heart:
with reason I prove to you.

You fool, why did you not consider
that you were made by God's hand,
exalted by him also
above every angel seated in Heaven
here seated on his throne?

Lucifer

Even on the throne will I sit,
(Let Lucifer attempt to go up to the throne)
and I will keep the same place
yet, in spite of you.

Both I and my comrades
will prove by sword
that I am more worthy
than the Father, indeed at all times.

Gabryell

Warnothans, myns es in Nef!
Gwren in kertha helly ef
Tha Effarn tha dewolgowe.

Ha why oll ye gowetha, 4v
Kewgh in kerth in weth gonȝa!
Crownkyowhe y gans clethythyowe!

Let them fight with swordys, and in the end Lucyfer voydeth and goeth downe to Hell, apariled fowle, with fyre abowt hem, turning to Hell, and every degre of devylls of lether and sprytys on cordys ruining into the playne and so remayne ther. Nine angells after Lucyfer goeth to Hell.

Lucyfer yn Hell

Owte, ellas, gallas fasowe!
Ythesaf in tewolgowe;
Ny allaf dos anotha.

In pytt downe ythof towles,
Abarth in Efarn kelmys
Gans chayne, tane a dro thymo.

Kyn nan bona lowenna,
Yma lower skynnys genaf
An elath sure tha drega.

321. Warnothans *this ed;* wanothans *MS.*
322. ef *this ed;* yef *MS.*
326 sd. ruining *this ed;* runing *MS;* running *Nance.*
327. gallas *this ed;* gallaf *MS.*
332. chayne, tane *MS;* chayne tane *Stokes.*
334. skynnys *(Nance);* skymys *MS;* skymnys *Stokes.*

Gabriel

At them, everyone in Heaven!
Let us drive him away
to Hell, to darkness.

And all you his comrades,
get away too with him!
Strike them with swords!

Let them fight with swords, and in the end Lucifer withdraws and goes down to Hell, horribly dressed, with fire around him, turning to Hell, and every degree of devils of leather and spirits on cords falling headlong into the place and so remain there. Nine angels after Lucifer goes to Hell.

Lucifer in Hell

O, alas, I have gone foul!
I am in darkness;
I cannot get out of it.

I am thrown into a deep pit,
bound inside Hell
with a chain, fire around me.

Although I have no joy
there are surely enough of the angels
fallen to live with me.

Deus Pater Gallas Lucifer, droke preve, 5r
Mes an Nef tha dewolgowe.
Ha lemyn un y lea ef
Me a vyn heb falladowe
Un dean formya

In valy Ebron, devery,
Rag collenwall aredy
An le may teth anotha.

Adam and Eva aparlet in whytt lether, in a place apoynted by the conveyour, and not to be sene tyll they be called, and then knell and ryse.

Dell ony onyn ha try,
Tas ha Mab in Trynytie,
Me a wra ge, dean, a bry,
Havall thagan face whare,

Haga wheth in y vody
Sperys, may hallas bewa;
Han bewnas pan an kelly
Ʒan doer te a dreyll arta.

Adam, save in ban in cloer,
Ha trayle ʒa gyke hatha owg.
Predar me thath wrill a thoer,
Havall ʒym then pen ha tros.

Myns es in tyre hag in moer,
Warnothans kymar gallus,
Yn serten, rag dry ascore,
Ty a vew may fota loose.

354. Predar *(Nance)*; preda *MS*.
355. ʒym ʒ^{m} *MS* (?); y^{m} *Stokes*.

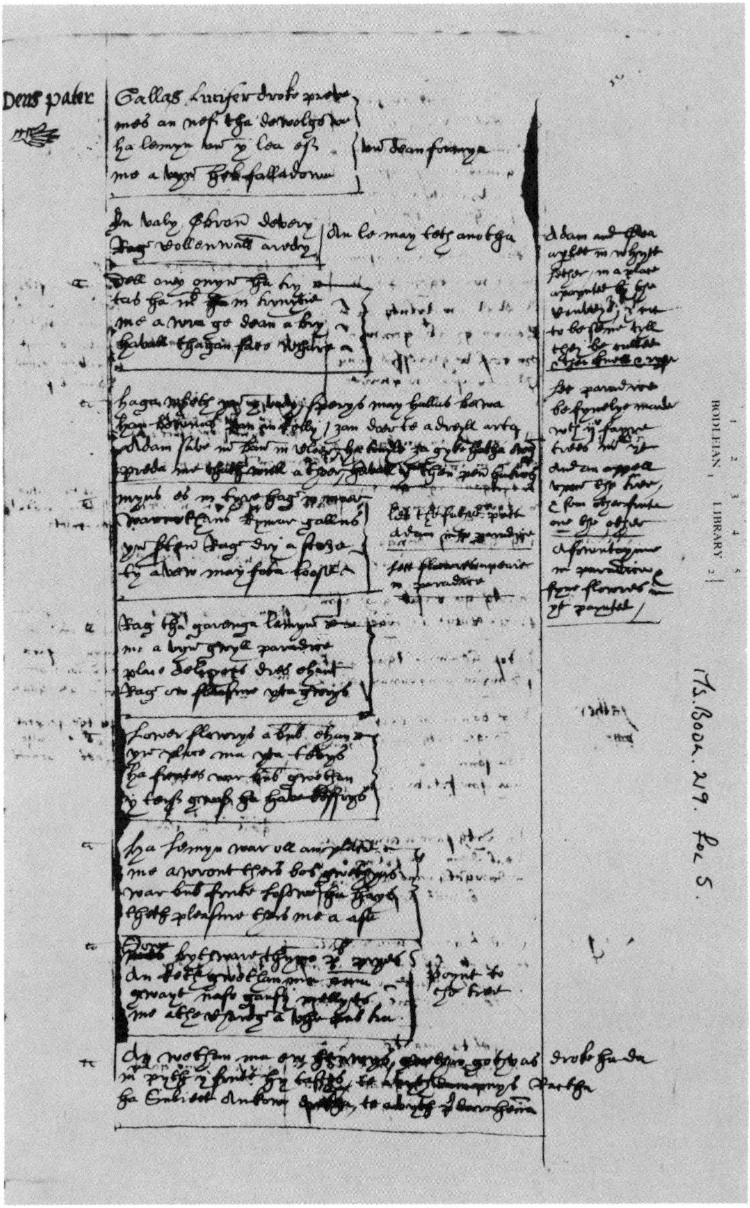

3. *The Creacion of the World*, MS Bodley 219, f4.

Deus Pater

Gone has Lucifer, vile snake,
out of Heaven to darkness.
And now in his place
without fail I will
make a man

in the valley of Hebron indeed
readily to fill
the place from which he came.

Adam and Eve dressed in white leather, in a place chosen by the conveyor, and not to be seen till they are called, and then kneel and rise.

As we are one and three,
Father and Son in Trinity,
I make you, man, from clay,
like to our face forthwith,

and I breathe into your body
a spirit, that you may live;
and when you lose life
to the earth you shall return.

Adam, stand up gently,
and turn to flesh and to blood.
Realise that I have made you of earth,
like to me from head to foot.

All that is in land and in sea,
take power over them.
To bring forth offspring, certainly,
you shall live till you be grey.

Let Paradice be fynelye made, with two fayre trees in yt; and an appell upon the Tree, and som other frute one the other.

A fowntayne in Paradice, and fyne flowres in yt paynted.

Rag tha garenga lemyn
Me a vyn gwyll Paradice,
Place delicyous dres ehan.
Rag ow fleasure yta gwrys!

Let the Father putt Adam into Paradice.

Lower flowrys a bub ehan,
Yn place ma yta tevys! *(Lett flowres apeare in Paradice)*
Ha frutes war bub gwethan
Y teyf gwaf ha have keffrys.

Ha lemyn, war oll an place
Me a wront theis bos gwethyas,
War bub frute; losowe ha hays
Theth pleasure theis me a ase.

Sowe bythware thymmo pub pryes
An keth gwethan ma omma *(poynt to the Tree)*
Gwayt nafe gansy mellyes,
Me athe chardg a uhe pub tra.

An wethan ma ew henwys
Gwethan gothvas droke ha da.
Mar pyth y frute hy tastys
Te a vyth dampnys ractha,
Ha subject Ankowe dretha.
Te a vyth, predar henna.

360 sd.1 *at 348 in MS.*
sd.2 *at 358 in MS.*
363 sd. *at 356 in MS.*
365 sd. *at 359 in MS.*

Let Paradise be finely made, with two fair trees in it; and an apple on the Tree, and some other fruit on the other.

A fountain in Paradise, and fine flowers painted in it.

Now for your love
I will make Paradise,
a place delicious beyond anything.
Behold it made for my pleasure! [*Paradise revealed*]

Let the Father put Adam into Paradise.

Plenty of flowers of every kind
see grown in this place! *(Let flowers appear in Paradise)*
And on every tree fruit
shall grow winter and summer likewise.

And now, over all the place
I allow you to be warden,
over every fruit; herbs and seeds
I leave to you for your pleasure.

But beware at all times
of this same tree here *(point to the Tree)*
Mind that it be not meddled with,
I charge you above everything.

This tree here is named
the Tree of Knowledge of Evil and Good.
If its fruit be tasted
you will be damned for it,
and subject to Death through it
you will be, consider that.

Tra morethack ew serten 5v
Gwellas Adam y honyn
Heb cowethas.

Adam, cuske tha ge lemyn:
A hanas tenaf ason
Me a vyn, ath tenewan,
Hag a honna pur serten
Me a vyn gwyll theis pryas.

Let the Father take a bone owt of Adam is syde.

Skon a wonyn ʒa asowe
Me a wra theʒa parowe
Pub ower thes rag ʒa weras.

Lett Adam laye downe and slepe wher Eva ys, and she by the conveyour must be taken from Adam is syde.

Adam A,a,a, ow Arluth da!
Benyn hy a vyth henwys.
Om corf ve gwressys honna:
Eva an ason ew gwryes.
Ragtha ythose benegas.

Lett fyshe of dyvers sortys apeare, and serten beastys, as oxen, kyne, shepe and such like.

Father Adam, yta an puskas,
Ethen in ayre, ha bestas
Kekeffrys in tyre ha more:

Ro thothans aga henwyn;
Y a the theth goribmyn.
Sav, na bashe ʒym war neb coore.

At the Father is comandement he ryseth.

389 sd. *at 385 in MS.*
402. a the theth *this ed;* a theth *MS;* a [thue] theth *Stokes.*
403. Sav *this ed;* Saw *MS.*
ʒym *this ed;* ʒm *MS;* y *Stokes.*
403 sd. *he this ed;* she *MS.*

It is indeed a sad thing
to see Adam by himself
without a companion.

Adam, sleep now:
from you a rib
I will take, from your side,
and surely from that
I will make you a wife.

Let the Father take a bone out of Adam's side.

At once from one of your ribs
I will make a mate for you
to help you always.

Let Adam lie down and sleep where Eve is, and she must be taken by the conveyor from Adam's side.

Adam

Oh,oh,oh, my good Lord!
She shall be called Woman.
You made her from my body:
Eve is made from my rib,
therefore are you blessed.

Let fish of divers sorts appear, and certain beasts, such as oxen, cattle, sheep and suchlike.

Father

Adam, see the fish,
birds in the air, and beasts
both in land and sea.

Give them their names;
they will come at your service.
Stand up, do not be in any way daunted.

At the Father's commandment he rises.

Adam

Yth henwaf bewgh ha tarow;
Oll an chattall debarowe
Aga henwyn kemerans.

Marth ha casak hag asan,
Ky ha cathe ha logosan,
Deffrans ehan ha serpentys.

A fyne serpent made with a virgyn face, and yolowe heare upon her head.

Let the serpent apeare, and also gees and hennes.

I rof henwyn than puskas:
Shewyan, pengarnas, selyas;
Me as recken oll dybblans.

Father

Rag bonas oll teake ha da
In whea dyth myns es formys,
Aga sona me a wra,
May fon sythvas dyth henwys
An dyth sure a bowesva
A bub dean a vo sylwys.
In dowhethyans a hena
Me a bowas desempys.

After the Father hath spoken, lett hem departe to Heaven in a clowde.

409 sd.2 *at 412 in MS.*
420 sd. *at 416 in MS.*

Adam

I name cow and bull;
let all the cattle
take their names individually.

Horse and mare and ass,
dog and cat and mouse,
various birds and snakes.

A fine serpent made with a maiden's face, and yellow hair upon her head.

Let the serpent appear, and also geese and hens.

I give names to the fish:
breams, gurnets, eels;
I take account of them all separately.

Father

Because all that has been made in six days
is fair and good,
I will bless them,
so that the seventh day may be called
the day of rest indeed
for every man who shall be saved.
In conclusion of that
I shall rest at once.

After the Father has spoken, let him depart to Heaven in a cloud.

Lucyfer

Gallas genaf hager dowle
Tha pytt Effarn mes an Nef.
Ena me a theke an rowle,
Ha lemyn in payne pur greif
    Y thesaf, a thewer nefra.

Nynges thymo remedy;
An trespas ytho mar vras.
Ny amownt whelas mercye;
Me a wore ny vyn an Tase
    Ow foly ȝymmo gava.

Rag henna, oll an vengens 6r
A allaf tha brederye
Me a vyn goneth dewhans,
Der neb for a vras envy;
    Ny wraf vry warbyn pewa.

My a wore yma formys
Gans an Tas yn dean a bry.
Havall thotha ythew gwryes,
Oll y gorffe in pur sembly.
    Ny allaf perthy henna.

Envyes ove war y bydn.
Me a vyn towlall neb gyn
    The dulla, mara callaf.

Gans Dew ythew apoyntes
Warden war oll Paradys.
Der henna ythof grevys:
Y wellas eve exaltys,
    Ha me dres ȝa yseldar.

Lucifer [*Emerging from Hell*] I have had a hideous fall
out of Heaven to the pit of Hell.
There I shall take the lead
and now I am in extreme pain
which lasts forever.

There is no remedy for me:
the sin was so great.
It does no good to seek mercy;
I know the Father will not
forgive me my folly.

Therefore I shall wreak all the vengeance
that I can think of
immediately,
by some way of great malice;
I don't care on whom.

I know there is a man formed
by the Father from clay.
He is made like Him,
all his body very beautifully.
I can't put up with that.

I bear a grudge against him.
I shall set some trap
to trick him if I can.

He is appointed by God
warden over all of Paradise.
That annoys me:
to see him exalted
and myself brought to humility.

Tha hena yma gwreghty,
Benyn yw henwys Eva.
Gwryes ay ason y fe hy,
Marthys teke a uhe pub tra,
    Saw y skeans yw brottall.

Me a vyn, mara callaf,
Whelas neb for the themtya,
    Pardel oma gwase suttall.

Now Adam ma ow lordya
Avell duke in Paradice,
Ha me sevyllyake omma
In Efarn yn tane, pub preyse
    In potvan bras ow lesky.

Sow an keth Adam yw gwryes
(Me a wore heb dowte in case)
Tha golenwall an romys
Es yn Nef der ow goth brase
    Avoyd, drethaf hawe mayny.

Sow mar callaf, der thavys,
Gwyll tha Adam thym cola,
Me an drossa tha baynes,
Na thefa then Nef nevera,
    Mar a mynna thym cola.

Sowe Eva manaf saya;
Hy ew esya tha dulla
    Es Adam, in gwyre ynta,
    Ha moy sympell.

461. potvan *Nance;* ponvan *MS;* powan *Stokes.*
475. *in margin of MS.*

That man has a wife,
a woman who is called Eve.
She was made from his rib,
marvellously lovely beyond everything,
but her wit is weak.

If I can, I shall
look for some way to tempt her,
subtle fellow that I am.

Now Adam is lording it
like a duke in Paradise,
and me a hanger-on here
in Hell in fire, always
burning in violent heat.

But that same Adam is made
(I know without any doubt)
to fill the places
that are empty in Heaven through my great pride,
through me and my followers.

But if, by a trick,
I can get Adam to listen to me,
I would bring him to pains,
so that he might never come to Heaven,
if he would listen to me.

But I shall try Eve;
she is easier to deceive
than Adam, certainly,
and more simple-minded.

In weth ny dale ȝym bos gwelys
Ow honyn in keth shapema.
Hager y thof defashes,
Ny yll tra bonas hackra:
    Why oll am gweall.

Belzabub Devill Hager lower os, me an vow! 6v
Yn myske oll an thewollow
    Nyges hackra.

Rag henna whela neb jyn,
Po an vyadg ny dale oye.
Eva thysa a theglyn
Mar uthicke pan wella hy
    Theth fegure yn kethe delma.

Let the Serpent walke in the playne.

Ha mar qwreta bargayne sure
Te a vith lower honorys
A wos Dew, kenthewa fure.
Yn forma mar pyth tullys
    Me a vyth compes ganso.

Lucyfer Na berth dowte, me an prevent,
Haga thro lower tha baynes;
    Me a levar ȝes fatla.

An Tas a rug der entent,
In myske oll prevas in bys,
Formya preve henwis Serpent;
Hag y thew wondrys fashes,
    Ȝa virgin deke pur havall.

Also I ought not to be seen
myself in this same shape.
I am horribly deformed,
nothing can be uglier:
you all see me.

Devil Beelzebub

You are ugly enough, I admit!
Amongst all the devils
there is none uglier.

So look for some plan,
or the venture will not be worth an egg.
Eve will shudder at you
when she sees your appearance so hideous
like this.

Let the Serpent walk in the place.

And if you make a firm bargain
you will be honoured enough
in spite of God, though he is wise.
If he is tricked in this way
I shall be even with him.

Lucifer

Have no fear, I shall worm my way in before him,
and bring enough to torments;
I will tell you how.

Amongst all the worms in the world,
the Father created on purpose
a snake named Serpent;
and it has a wonderful face,
very like a fair maiden.

Sottall ythew gans henna,
A ughe beast na preif in bys.
Yn henna manaf entra,
Ha prevathe tha Baradice
    Me avyn mos heb fyllall.

Kynna wore hy cowse banna
Me as rowle hy del vannaf,
Ha kyns es dos a lena
Tha Adam ha tha Eva
    Me a wra neb enfugy.

Torpen Devyll

Gwra in della, me ath pys,
Par dellostȧ jǫwle wylly.
Mar qwreth henna, honorys
Ty a vyth bys venarye,
Ha pen rowler warnan ny
    Heb dowt in case.

Lucyfer

By and by thow shalt se that;
Ha pur uskes gwraf an pratt
    Then Serpent, in spyte thy face.

Let Lucyfer com to the Serpent and offer to goe in to her. The Serpent voydeth. And stayeth, and ofereth to go in to her.

Ay! Redeball dowethy!
Gorta ha byth thym rowlys!
Gas ve tha entra agye,
Rag ty ny vethys dowtyes
    Drefan y bosta mar deke.

520 sd. *voydeth. And stayeth, and* *this ed;* *voydeth and stayeth and* *[Lucifer again]* *Stokes.*

It is subtle as well,
above any animal or snake in the world.
I will enter into it,
and privately to Paradise
I will sneak without fail.

Though she does not know how to speak
a bit
I shall control her as I wish,
and before coming away
I shall do some harm
to Adam and to Eve.

Devil Torpen Do so, I entreat you,
sly devil that you are.
If you do that
you will be honoured for ever,
and head ruler over us
without a doubt.

Lucifer You shall see that right away;
and I shall very quickly play the trick
on the Serpent, in spite of her
face.

Let Lucifer come to the Serpent and attempt to enter her. The Serpent withdraws. And he detains her, and attempts to enter her.

Hey! Curse you!
Stop and be ruled by me!
Let me get inside,
for you will not be feared
because you are so lovely.

Lucyfer entreth into the Serpent.

Ty a vyth yntertaynes
Ha gans Eva sure cregys;
Thyth fysmant ȝethy a bleake.

Aban oma close entrys
Unas sche, a barth agye,
Ow voice oll yta changys,
A vel mayteth in tevery.
Me ne vethaf confethes
Ombos ynaff fallsurye;
Sottall lower ove, me agreys.

Let Eva walke in Paradice.

Hag a vyn mos, heb gwill gycke, 7r
In wethan pur smoth, heb mycke,
A vell eall wheak afynes.

The Serpent singeth in the Tree.

Eva

Me a vyn mos tha wandra
Omma yn myske an flowrys.
Oll pub pleasure an bysma
Yn plasma yta tevys,
May thew confort ȝa wellas.

Serpent in the Tree

Eva, praga na theta nes,
Rag cowse orthaf ha talkya?
Un dra a won om gothvas -
Pur lowenake am gwressa
Cola orthaf a mennas.

4. *The Fall of Man*, panel 7 of *The Creation Window*.

Lucifer enters the Serpent.

You will be accepted
and certainly believed by Eve;
your face will please her.

Since I have entered close
within you, inside,
see, my voice is all changed,
just like a maiden.
I shall not be discovered
to have any falsehood in me;
I am subtle enough, I believe.

Let Eve walk in Paradise.

And I will go without making a sound
smoothly into the tree, without noise,
dressed up like a sweet angel.

The Serpent sings in the Tree.

Eve

I shall go wandering
here amongst the flowers.
Every delightful thing of the world
see grown in this place,
so that it is a pleasure to behold.

Serpent in the Tree

Eve, why do you not come near,
to talk with me and chat?
One thing I know from my knowledge -
it would make me very happy
if you would listen to me.

Then Eva wondreth of the Serpent when she speaketh.

Eva

Pew ostashe es in wethan
A wartha gans troes ha cane?
Marth yw genaf thath clowas.

Lett Eva looke stranglye on the Serpent when she speakethe.

Worthys me nembes nygys,
Na byle os devethys:
Marth ew genaf tha wellas.

Serpent

Na gymmar marth vyth, benynvas.
Me a theth a thewheʒas
Mes an Neif gans hast pur vras,

Rag cowsall theis a henna
Omma lemyn pur brevath.
Me athe pys, awos neb tra
Na gymar marth anotha,
Na owne vyth es ow gwellas.

Eva

Nynges owne thym a hanas,
Drefan bose mar deake tha face,
Na whath dowt vetholl in bys,

Rag der tha ere yth falsa
Ty tha thos an Nef totheta,
Ha mara tethe a lena
Pur welcom y those genaf,
Ha thawell ythe fythe cregys.

552 sd. *at 557 in MS.*

Then Eve wonders at the Serpent when she speaks.

Eve

Who are you in the tree,
with noisy song above?
I am amazed to hear you.

Let Eve look coldly at the Serpent when she speaks.

I have no business with you
nor where you have come from:
I am amazed to see you.

Serpent

Do not be amazed at all, madam.
I have just come
out of Heaven in a very great hurry,

in order to speak to you about that
now, very privately here.
I beg you, on no account
be amazed at it,
nor take fright at all at the sight of me.

Eve

I have no fear of you,
because your face is so lovely,
nor yet any terror at all,

For it would seem from your statement
that you have come hastily from Heaven,
and if you come from there
you are most welcome to me,
and the better you will be trusted.

Eva talketh famylyarlye with the
Serpent and cometh neare hem.

Lavar thybma thathe negys,
Ha mar callaf tha weras,
Na berth dowt, ny vyth nehys.

Serpent

Ow nygys a dreyle tha les
Mar a mynta ow krysye.
Saw yma thym a hanas
Dowte pur vras a anfugye
Mara qwrees ow dyskyvera.

Eva

Na vannaf tha theskyvra,
Ow hothman, a tra in bys.
Rag henna, meare tha volta,
Ty a yll gule tha negys,
Ha ow threst yw y vos da.

Serpent

Da cotha; yw, na thowt perill, 7v
War ow honesty, benyn vas.
Pokeean y whressan fyllall,
Hag y fea peth pur vras
Ha me gweffe tha vos punyshes.

Eva

Why a lavar gwyre, dremas,
Henna vea hager dra.
Yma thymma hyrathe bras
Rag gothevas pandra vea!
In cutt termyn ages negys
Cowsow, I praya!

571 sd. *at 574 in MS.*
571. *Marginal note* Gen: 3
575. krysye *this ed;* kysye *MS;* kyfye *Stokes.*

Eve talks familiarly with the Serpent and comes near him.

Tell me your business,
and if I can help you
it will not be denied, have no fear.

Serpent

My business will turn to your profit
if you will believe me.
But I have
very great fear of trouble from you
lest you betray me.

Eve

I shall not betray you,
my friend, for anything in the world.
So, to speak very boldly,
you can do your business,
and my trust is that it is good.

Serpent

It is good (it ought to be!), do not fear danger,
upon my honour, madam.
Otherwise I should be acting wrongly,
and it would be a very great sin
and me worthy to be punished.

Eve

You speak truly, sir,
that would be a horrible thing.
I have a great longing
to know what it could be!
Please tell me
the news at once.

Serpent

Me a levar thys, Eva,
Ha coole orthaf os ehan.
Maga fure te a vea,
Avel Dew es awartha.
Haga uffya pub tra.

Eva

Myhall! Sera, thewgh gramercy!
A callen dos then pryckna
Y thalsan bos pur very.
Henna vea reall dra,
Bos cooth ȝa Thew awarȝa
Ha in pub poynt equall gonsa,
Ha maga fure acomptys.

Yn erna, re sent, deffry,
Yth halsan rowlya pur gay,
Ha bos stately ȝom devyse.

Y praytha, lavar fatla,
Perthy ny allaf pella!
Me a vyth sure tha lacka
Mes te thym a lavara
En by and by.

Skeans benyn ew brottall,
Ha me nygof over sottall.
Lavar thym kyns es hythy,
Me athe pyese, an nowethys!

608. rowlya *Stokes;* rowtya *MS.*

Serpent

I will tell you, Eve,
and listen to me at all costs.
You would be as wise
as God above,
and know everything.

Eve

Michael! Sir, thank you!
If I could come to that point
I could be very happy.
That would be a splendid thing,
to be on familar terms with God above
and equall to him in every way,
and considered to be as wise.

Then, by the saint, truly,
I could rule most brilliantly,
and be dignified according to my wish.

Please, say how,
I can wait no longer!
I shall certainly be the worse
unless you tell me
at once.

Woman's wit is weak,
and I am not particularly subtle.
Tell me the news
at once, I beg you!

Serpent

Me a levar thys, Eva.
Mar qwreth tastya an frute ma
Es oma war an wethan,

Maga fure te a vea
A vell Dew es awartha
In Nef uhall a uhan.
Gow vyth ny lavaraf.

Let Eva looke angerly on the
Serpent and profer to departe.

Eva

What! Ew hena tha thevyse!
Tam vyth ny vyth cregys,
Henna me a levar theis,
Theth cussyllyow in poyntna,
Me a levar theis praga.

Dew a ornas contrarye:
Na thesan tastya henna.
Hay gommandement pur thefry
A rose straytly, dres pub tra,
Na wrellan mellya worty.
Prag y whreth genaf flattra?

Serpent

Golsow, golsow, Eva, ha des nes; 8r
Shame ew genaf tha glowas
Ow cregy then gyrraw na.

Praga, me a levar thies,
Y wruge Dew ry an chardgna?
Genas a peva tastys,
Maga fure te a vea
Yn pub poynt sure a vella.

Serpent

I will tell you, Eve.
If you taste this fruit
that is here on the tree

you would be as wise
as God who is above
in Heaven high above us.
I tell no lie.

Let Eve look angrily at the Serpent and make as if to leave.

Eve

What! Is that your idea!
Your advice on that matter
will not be a bit believed,
I tell you that.
I shall tell you why.

God has commanded the opposite:
that we were not to taste that.
And in truth he gave his commandment
strictly, above everything else,
that we should not meddle with it.
Why are you wheedling me?

Serpent

Listen, Eve, listen, and come close;
I am sorry to hear you
believing those words.

Why, I say to you,
did God give that order?
If it were tasted by you,
you would surely be as wise
as him in every way.

An Tas, ef ny vynsa sure
Worthe dean vetholl bos mar fure
Tha othvas a droke ha da.

Rag henna, benynvas Eva,
Genas ny vannaf flattra
Na ny vanaf usya gowe.

Kooll ge thym men tha gesky,
Mar mynta bos exaltys:
Poken sertayne venarye
Why a vyth a vell flehys.
Bo yn assentys te a glow,
Eva gentill.

Eva Yea, yea, me a glowe.
Hag a rose ʒym chardge mar strayte
Me an byth payne ha gallarowe
Mara qwren terry un iect
Y gomanndement thyn reyse.

Par hap in Efarne neffra
Ny an bythe agen trygva,
Mar ny vyth y vothe sewyes.

Serpent Taw, taw, Eva, ythos foole,
Ny vynnys cola orthe da.
Me a ragtha, ty an owle
Ow husyll mar qwreth naha.
Genas nygof contentys.

656. gentill gentll *MS*.

The Father, he certainly would not want
any man at all to be so wise
as to know about evil and good.

So, madam Eve,
I will not wheedle you
nor will I use a lie.

Listen to me strongly urging you,
if you want to be exalted,
otherwise for certain forever
you will be like children.
Or you will listen obediently,
sweet Eve.

Eve Yes, yes, I will listen.
And he gave me an order so strict
that I shall have pain and agony
if I should break one jot
of his commandment given us.

Perhaps in Hell for ever
we shall have our home,
if his will is not obeyed.

Serpent Hush, hush, Eve, you are a fool,
you will not listen to good.
I vouch for it, you will repent it
if you ignore my advice.
I am not pleased with you.

Na vea me theth cara,
Ny vynsan theth cossyllya
Tha vos bargayne mar vras gwryes.

She commethe neare the Serpent agayne and geveth heed to his words.

Eva

A cuffan y voȝa gwyre,
Me a sewsya tha thesyre,
Drefan te tha thos an Nef.

Serpent

Why a levar gwyre, benynvas,
Ny ryse thewh ow mystrustya:
An Nef ny the mes tues vas;
Me ew onyn an sortna.
Rewhy ran thages dremas,
Po an vyadge ny dale tra,
Mes y bart ef an geffa.

Eva

Ny vannaf bos mar grefnye
Tha wetha oll ow honyn.
Adam sure dres pub hunyth
Me an kare, po Dew defan
The wetha heb y shara.

Serpent

Me a ysten an skoran; 8v
Kymmar an frute annethy.

Let the Serpent bow downe the appell to Eva, and she takethe the appell.

Eva

Me ara in pur serten.
Ny allaf na pell perthy,
Pan vo reys tastya anothy.

689 sd. *at 680 in MS.*
appell appll *MS.*

Were it not that I love you
I would not advise you
that so great a bargain was to be had.

She comes near the Serpent again and gives heed to his words.

Eve

If I knew this were true
I would conform to your wish,
since you have come from Heaven.

Serpent

You say true, madam,
there is no need for you to distrust me;
only good people come from Heaven:
I am one of that sort.
Give some to your husband,
or the venture will be worthless,
unless he gets his share.

Eve

I will not be so greedy
as to keep it all myself.
Truly above everyone
I love Adam, or God forbid -
to keep him without his share!

Serpent

I will hold out the branch;
take the fruit from it.

Let the Serpent bow down the apple to Eve, and she takes the apple.

Eve

I will indeed.
I can no longer refrain,
since it must be tasted.

Serpent

Nefra na gybmar dowte,
Te a yll bos pur verry.
Gans tha lagasowe a lees
Ty a weall pub tra omma,
Ha pur fure te a vyth gwryes,
Evell Dew; na thowt henna,
Eva, me a levar thyes.

Na vea me theth cara,
Ny vynsan a wos neb tra
Yn ban tha vos exaltys.

Eva

Mear a rase thewhy, sera,
Ow ry cusyll ȝym mar stowte.
Orthowh me a vyn cola,
Ha, by God, nynges ȝym dowte
Tha dastya an keth avall.

Haw dremas a wor thym grace
Tha weyll vyadge mar nobell,
Ha, re Thew an Drengys Tase,
Ef am sett yn ban uhall,
Hagam gormall meare, heb dowt.

Serpent

Ke in ker, Eva benynvas,
Te a yll gothvas thym grace
Rag an vyadge.

Hag Adam, dell ew dremas,
A hanas a wra pur vras.
An bargayn ny vyth eddrack.

707. an *Nance;* a *MS.*
709. nobell nobll *MS.*

Serpent

Never fear,
you can be very happy.
You will see everything here
with your eyes open,
and you will be made very wise,
like God; do not doubt that,
Eve, I tell you.

Were it not that I love you,
on no account would I wish
you to be exalted on high.

Eve

Many thanks to you, sir,
for giving me such sound advice.
I will listen to you,
and, by God, I have no hesitation
in tasting this apple.

And my husband will give me thanks
for undertaking so noble a venture,
and, by God the Father in Trinity,
he will set me up high,
and will doubtless praise me greatly.

Serpent

Go your way, madam Eve,
you may thank me
for the venture.

And Adam, good man as he is,
will make very much of you.
There will be no regretting the bargain.

Eva

Farewell, ow hothman an Nef;
Me ath kare bys venary.
Tha Adam kerras pur greyf
Me a vyn, the sallugye,
    Han avall y presentya.

Eva departeth to Adam and presenteth hem the appell.

Serpent

Gwra yn della, me ath pys.
Ty a glow keen nawothow
    Kyns ow gwellas ve arta.

Eva

Adam, Adam, pythesta?
Golsow thymmo ha des neese.
Yma genaf theth pleycya -
Na barth dowt a bratt es gwryes
    May woffas thym grassowe.

Adam

Welcom, Eva, os, benynvas.
Marsew an nowothow da
Ty a vythe rewardyes,
Ham hollan yn weth ganȝa
    Te a vyth prest theth plegadow.

Eva

(Shew the appell to Adam) Merowgh, merowgh orth hemma! 9r
Tomma gay a avall theys!
Mar qwreth tastya anotha
Eve a drayle theȝo tha leas,
    Moy ees myllow a bynsowe.

723 sd. *appell* appll *MS.*

Eve

Farewell, my friend from Heaven;
I shall love you for ever.
I shall go boldly to Adam,
to greet him,
and to present the apple.

Eve departs to Adam and presents him the apple.

Serpent

Do so, please.
You will hear other news
before seeing me again.

Eve

[*Calling*] Adam, Adam, where are you?
Listen to me and come close.
I have something to please you -
do not be afraid of trick's being played -
so that you should thank me.

Adam

[*Coming forward*] You are welcome, madam Eve.
If the news is good
you will be rewarded,
and you shall have my heart as well too
ready at your pleasure.

Eve

(Show the apple to Adam) Look, look at this!
See what a lovely apple for you!
If you taste it
it will turn to profit for you,
more than thousands of pounds.

Adam

Des nes, gas ve thy wellas
Mara sewa avall da.
Lavar peveva kefys.

Adam is afrayde of the syght of the appell.

Eva

Praga, Adam, ow fryas,
Der dowte es thyes y wellas?
Lavar ȝymmo, me ath pyes.

Adam

Ny bleig thym sight anotha.
Dowt pur vras yma thyma.
Nagewa vas, me a gryes.

Ty mar pe hemma terrys
Mes an wethan defennys
Ragtha me a vyth grevys.

Eva

Neffra na thowt a henna,
Adam wheak, ow harenga.
Me a levar thys, mar pleage,
Yn pan vanar ym bema.

Sera, ha me ow qwandra,
Me a glowas a wartha
War an weathan udn eal wheake
Sure ow cana.

Me am be wondrys fancye
Orth y wellas in weathan.
Ha thevy in curtessye
Y profyas, avell cothman,
Mere a dacklow, rom lowta,
Ha pur worthy.

757. *Tail-rhyme in MS.*

Adam

Come close, let me see
if it is a good apple.
Tell me where it was found.

Adam is afraid at the sight of the apple.

Eve

Why, Adam, my husband,
are you really afraid to see it?
Tell me, please.

Adam

The sight of it does not please me.
I am very much afraid.
I believe it is not good.

If you have picked this
from the forbidden tree
I shall be sorry for it.

Eve

Never be afraid about that,
dear Adam, my love.
I will tell you, if it will please,
by what means I got it.

Sir, as I was wandering,
I heard above
on the tree a sweet angel
surely singing.

I had a strange delight
from seeing him in the tree.
And courteously to me,
like a friend, he offered
many things, on my faith,
very honourable things too.

Adam

A Eva, Eva, ty a fyllas,
Ow cola orthe an eal na.
Droke polat o, me a gryes,
Neb a glowses owe cana,
  Ha athe cossyllas tha derry
  An avall na.

Eva

Sera, eve a gowsys ȝym mar deake,
Ny wothyan tabm y naha.
Hay bromas o mar wheake,
May wruge eve thyma cola.
  Ny thowtys, war ow ena,
  A falsurye.

Hay bromas y tho largya:
Mar qwrean tastya an frutna
A vell Dew ny a vea,
  Ha maga fure.

My a fylly in urna
A callen dos then prickna
  Y fea bargayn pur fuer.

Adam

A, owte, owt warnas, Eva!
Me a yll cussya henna!
Towles on tha vyshew bras,
  Ha worthy the gemeras.

Hena o hagar vargayne, 9v
Eva, me a lavar theis.
Nebas lowre a vyth an gwayne
Pan vo genas cowle connptys.
  Soweth, aylaas!

772. Ha *this ed;* Na *MS;* hag *Stokes.*

Adam

Oh Eve, Eve, you have done wrong
in listening to that angel.
He was a bad lot, I believe,
whom you heard singing,
and who advised you to pick
that apple.

Eve

Sir, he spoke to me so nicely,
I did not know how to deny him anything.
And his promise was so sweet,
that he made me listen.
Upon my soul, I was not afraid
of treachery.

And his promise was so generous:
if we were to taste that fruit
we would be like God,
and as wise.

It seemed to me then
if I could get to that point
it would be a very great bargain.

Adam

Oh out, out upon you, Eve!
I may well curse that!
We are fallen into great trouble,
and worthy to have it.

That was an ugly bargain,
I tell you, Eve.
Little enough will be the gain
when you have fully counted it.
Woe, alas!

Eva *(Profer the appell to Adam. He refuseth yt)* Taw, Adam, na vyth serrys;
Ny theth droke whath anotha.
An keth perill yth towtyes,
Haga laverys thotha
    Oll an perill in pub poynte.

Saw eve thema a wrontyas
Nago thema dowte in case,
    War y perill, wondrys coynt.

Adam A, molath then horsen kam,
Ha thage in weth ganso!
Ny an gevyth sure droke lam
Rag tha veadge in torn ma,
    Ha worthy ȝa gawas blame.

Eva *(Lett her speak angerly to Adam)* Yea,
    yea, me an gevyth oll an blame
Tha worthis ge lemyn Adam,
    Pynagell for ytha an game.

Saw a pony dewyow gwryes
Ny veas malbew serrys,
    Me a wore hena ynta.

Adam Taw, taw, na vyth ȝymmo mar ucky.
An Serpent o re wylly
    Ragas she in keth tornma.

811. Pynagell pynagll *MS.*

Eve — *(Offer the apple to Adam. He refuses it)* Hush, Adam, do not be angry;
evil has not come from it yet.
I was afraid of the same danger,
and told him
all the danger in every detail.

But he guaranteed me
on his peril, most artfully,
that there was nothing in the matter for me to be afraid of.

Adam — O, curse the evil bastard,
and you too with him!
We shall certainly have disaster
because of your dealings on this occasion,
and are worthy to have blame.

Eve — *(Let her speak angrily to Adam)* Yes, yes, I shall get all the blame
from you now, Adam,
however the game goes.

But if we were made Gods
you wouldn't be a damn bit angry,
I know that well.

Adam — Hush, hush, please do not be so silly.
The Serpent was too cunning
for you on this occasion.

Ev a brofyas lowre gow theis,
Ha genas ymons cregys.
Owe gyrryow a vyth prevys
May fyth lowre payne ractha.

Eva Yea, y thosta ge dean fure,
Ny vynny orthaf cola.
Mar ny vethaf ow desyre
Neffra nyn gwellyth omma,
Methaf, un spyes.
Lett her profer to depart.

An eal ega in wethan
Y cowses gyrryow efan,
Ha me an creys.

Syr, war nebas lavarowe,
Tast gy part an avallowe,
Po ow harenga ty a gyll.

Meir, kymar an avall teake *(profer hem the appell)*
Po sure inter te hath wreage
An garenga quyt a fyll,
Mar ny vynyth y thebbry.

Adam Henna ythew trewath dra,
Aban reys ȝymmo cola
Po kelly an garensa
Es ornys interrannye.

823. vynny *this ed;* vynnys *MS.*
825. gwellyth *(Nance);* gwellaf *MS.*
826. Methaf *(Nance);* methan *MS.*
833 sd. *appell* appll *MS.*

He offered a lot of lies to you,
and you believe them.
My words will prove true
in that there will be sufficient
punishment for it.

Eve Yes, you are a wise man,
you do not want to listen to me.
If I do not get my way
you will never see me here
once, I say.
Let her make as if to leave.

The angel that was in the tree
spoke plain words,
and I believe him.

In short, sir,
taste a part of the apples,
or you will lose my love.

Look, take the nice apple *(offer him the apple)*
or else the love between you and your wife
will certainly fail utterly,
if you will not eat it.

Adam That is a sad thing,
when I must obey
or lose the love
that is established between us.

Eva gentill, navyth serrys, 10r
Me ara oll del vynny.
Drova thymo desempys,
Ha me ara ye thebbrye.

Eva *(Eva gevethe hem the appell)* Yea,
gwra thym indella;
Drevon bew ow harenga
Ty a vyth bys venarye.

Meer an avall ma omma:
Kymar ha debar tothta,
Dowt me genas tha serry.

Adam receveth the appell, and doth tast yt, and so repenteth and throweth yt awaye.

Adam Ogh, ogh, trew, ny re behas,
Ha re dorras an deffen.
A teball benyn heb grace,
Ty rom tullas ve heb kene!

Agen corfow nooth gallas,
Mere, warnan pub tenewhan!
Om gwethan ny gans deel glase
Agen prevetta pur glose.

Y whon gwyre Dew agen Tas
Y sor thyn y teig pur vras.
Me an suppose.

841. gentill gentll *MS*.
845 sd. *appell* appll *MS*.
851 sd. *appell* appll *MS*.

Dear Eve, do not be angry,
I will do everything as you wish.
Bring it to me at once,
and I will eat it.

Eve *(Eve gives him the apple)* Yes,
do so for my sake;
you will be my love for ever,
as long as I live.

See this apple here:
take and eat quickly,
lest I be angry with you.

Adam receives the apple, and tastes it, and so repents and throws it away.

Adam Oh, oh, misery, we have sinned
and have broken the prohibition.
Oh, graceless, evil woman,
you have tricked me without reason!

Our bodies have become naked
all over, look!
Let us cover our private parts
very secretly with green leaves.

I know well that God our Father
will visit his anger upon us very heavily.
I am sure of it.

Meere, mere, an gwelta, Eva?
Yma ef ow toos omma.
Rag meth, dean ny a lemma
    Tha gutha in tellar close.

Eva loketh upon Adam very stranglye and spekethe every thing.

Father
Adam, Adam, pandra wreth?
Prag ny theth thom welcomma?

Adam
Drefan ow bos nooth heb qweth,
Ragas y theth tha gutha
    Yn tellar ma.

Fig leaves redy to cover ther members.

Father
Pyw a thysqwethas thyso
Tha vos noth tryes corf ha bregh,
Lemyn an frute grace navo
Monas the thibbry heb peyghe?
    Prag y wresta in della?

Adam
Thyma ve why a rose gwreag:
Hona yw oll tha vlamya.
Hy a dorras an avall teake
Hagan dros thym tha dastya.

865 sd. *at 861 in MS.*
spekethe every thing spekethe euy thing *MS; speketh [not] eny thing Stokes.*

[God approaches.]

Look, look, do you see him, Eve?
He is coming here.
Let us go away from here for shame,
to hide in a secret place.

Eve looks upon Adam very coldly and says everything.

[They hide from God.]

Father

Adam, Adam, what are you doing?
Why do you not come to welcome me?

Adam

[speaking while hidden] Because I am naked without clothing,
I went and hid from you
in this place.

Fig leaves to cover their members.
[Adam and Eve emerge wearing fig-leaves.]

Father

Who has told you
that you are naked feet, body and arm,
unless it was the fruit which you were not permitted
to go and eat without sin?
Why have you done so?

Adam

You gave me a wife:
she is all to blame.
She picked the sweet apple
and brought it to me to taste.

Father

A ban golsta orty hy,
Ha gwythyll dres ow defan,
In wheys lavyr tha thybbry
Ty a wra bys yth worffan.
Eva, prag y wresta gye
Tulla tha bryas heb ken?

Eva

An Serpent der falsurye 10v
An temptyas tha wuthell hena,
Hag y promysyas tha vee
Y fethan tha well neffra.
    Hemma yw gwyre.

Father

Rag ty tha gulla ortye,
Ha tulla tha bryas leell,
Nefra gostyth thy gorty
Me a ordayne bos benyn;
    Trust gy thom gear.

May moyghea y lavyer hy
Der weyll ow gorhemen troghe,
Na heb mear lavyer defry
Benytha nystevyth floghe.

(The Father speketh to the Serpent)

Prag y wresta, malegas,
Lavar, aga thulla y?

Serpent

Me a lavar theis an case:
Rag bos dethy joy mar vras,
    Ha me pub ere ow lesky.

885. *Tail-rhyme in MS.*
897. ow *conj. Stokes;* O *MS.*

Father

Since you listened to her,
and acted against my order,
you will eat in sweated labour
right until the end.
Eve, why did you
deceive your husband without reason?

Eve

The Serpent treacherously
tempted me to do it,
and he promised me
that we should be the better always.
This is the truth.

Father

Because you listened to him,
and deceived your faithful husband,
I ordain that woman shall be
always subject to her man;
mark my words.

So that her labour may increase
through breaking my commandment,
not without great labour indeed
shall she ever bear a child.

(The Father speaks to the Serpent)
Cursed one, tell me,
why did you deceive them?

Serpent

I will tell you why it was:
because of their having such great joy,
and me continually burning.

Father

Serpent, rag aga themptya,
Mer a bayne es thyes ornys.
Malegas os dres pub tra,
Ha dreis preif ha beast in bys.

Owne a hanas rag neffra
Dean an gevyth prest pub preis.
Ha te, preif, a wra cruppya,
Ha slynckya war doer a heys.

Ynter ye hays hy ha tee
Me a wra envy neffra.
Ha henna theth pedn ʒa gy
Than doer sure a wra crushya.

Lett Lucyfer come owte of the Serpent (the Serpent remayneth in the Tree).
And lett hem crepe on his belly to Hell with great noyse.

Lucyfer the Serpent

Attoma hager vyadge,
May hallaf kyny ellas.
Yth om brovas gwan dyacke,
May thof poyntyes ʒa bayne bras,
Tha pytt Efarn, ow cheif place.

916. crushya *this ed;* cruppya *MS;* croppya *Stokes*.
917sd. *come* cōm *MS*.

Father

Serpent, for tempting them,
much pain is ordained for you.
You are cursed beyond everything,
both beyond every snake and beast in the world.

Man shall always have
fear of you all the time.
And you shall creep, snake,
and slink along the ground.

Between her seed and you
I shall cause eternal hatred.
and that shall surely
crush your head to the ground.

Let Lucifer come out of the Serpent (the Serpent remains in the Tree). And let him creep on his belly to Hell with great noise.

Lucifer the Serpent

Here is a nasty business,
I may well bewail it.
I have proved myself a bad worker,
and I'm appointed to great pain,
in the pit of Hell, my headquarters.

Me a vyn dallath cruppya,
Ha slyncya war doer a heys.
Tham shape ow honyn ytoma
Why a weall, oma treylys,
    Drog pullat ha brase.

Kynnam boma lowena,
An chorle Adam, hag Eva,
Tha Effarn y towns thymmo,
Haga asshew, rag neffra,
    Poyntys der ganawe an Tas.

Han Serpent tregans yna. 11r
Nefra nythe a lena,
    Rag ythew malegas bras.

Adam A Dase, Dew athe wullowys,
Aban ove tha throke towlys,
Grannt theth creatour, me ath pys,
    Na pyth a Oyle a Vercy.

Father Adam, kyns es dewath an bys
Me a wront Oyle Mercye theis,
    Ha tha Eva theth wrethtye.

923. slyncya *so MS.*
937. Grannt *this ed;* graunt *Stokes; MS either.*
creatour creato' *MS;* creator *Stokes.*
938. pyth p^{t} *MS;* part *Stokes.*

I will start to crawl,
and slink along the ground.
Here I am turned, you see,
to my own shape,
a great evil fellow.

Although I'm unhappy,
that wretch Adam, and Eve,
they will come to me in Hell,
and their offspring, for ever,
ordered by the mouth of the Father.

And let the Serpent stay there.
It will never come from there,
for it is greatly cursed.

[*Crawls into Hell*]

Adam Oh Father, God in your light,
since I am thrown into sin,
grant your creature, I beg you,
some of the Oil of Mercy.

Father Adam, before the end of the world
I will grant you the Oil of Mercy,
and to Eve your wife.

Sow, pur wyre, thymo ve creis,
Worth tha wreak drefan cola
Rag terry an keth frutes
A wrug defenna ʒa wortes,
Spearn y teg thym ha speras,
Han earbes an keth dorna
Ty a thebar in tha wheys
Theth vara, pur wyre nefra,
Arna veys arta treyles
An keth doer kyns a wrugaf:
A thowst omma y feus gwryes,
Hatha thowst y theth arta.

Let the Father assend to Heaven.

Adam

Theth voth rebo collenwys,
Arluth Nef han byes keverys.
Me a yll bos lowanheys,
Kyns es bos dewath an bys,
  Cawas an Oyle a Vercy.

Kynthew paynes ow cortas
In Effarn in neb place,
Ny ew neb an dendyllas
  Drefan an defan terry.

Father in Heaven

Mehall, yskydnyow, eall splan,
Hellowgh Adam gans cletha dan,
  Hay wreag, mes a Baradice.

Ha deaw gweth dothans gwra doen,
Thaga hutha pub season,
  Aga noothe navo gwellys.

But, in truth, believe me,
because you obeyed your wife,
for picking the very fruits
that I forbade you,
the ground shall bear thorns and briars,
and the plants of that ground
you shall eat in your sweat
for your bread, for ever in truth,
until you have turned again
to the same earth that I first created.
From dust here you were made,
and to dust you will return.

Let the Father ascend to Heaven.

Adam

Thy will be done,
Lord of both Heaven and earth.
I may be gladdened,
before the end of the world,
to obtain the Oil of Mercy.

Though pains are pending
somewhere in Hell,
it is we who have deserved it
through breaking the commandment.

Father in Heaven

Go down, Michael, bright angel,
drive Adam and his wife
out of Paradise with a sword of fire.

And take two garments to them,
to cover them all seasons,
that their nakedness be not seen.

Mychaell in Heaven

Arluth, me a wra henna.
Parys yw genaf pub tra
    Tha vose thothans a lemma.

Desend Angell .

Cherubyn

Adam, ke in mes an wlase,
Tha greys an bys tha vewa;
Te tha honyn tha ballas,
Theth wreag genas tha netha.
Two garmentys of skynnes to be geven to Adam and Eva by the Angell.
Adam, attoma dyllas,
Hag Eva, thages qwetha.
    Fystenowgh, bethans gweskes.
Receave the garmentys.
Fystenowgh trohan daras, 11v
Rag omma ny wrewgh trega. *(Let them depart owt of Paradice, and Adam and Eva folowing them)*
Ages tooles tha ballas,
Hages pegans tha netha
    Y towns parys.

Let them putt on the garmentys and shewe a spade and a dystaf.

972 sd. *at 968 in MS.*
975 sd. *so placed in Stokes; at 972 in MS.* *Two* ij *MS; The Stokes.*
981. tha *Stokes;* that *MS.*
983 sd. *spade this ed;* spyndell *MS.*

Michael in Heaven

I will do so, Lord.
I have everything ready
to go from here to them.

Angel descend.

Cherub

Adam, go out of the land,
to live in the middle of the world;
you yourself to dig,
your wife to spin.

Two garments of hide to be
given to Adam and Eve by the Angel.

Adam, here is raiment,
and Eve, clothing for you.
Hurry, let them be worn.

Receive the garments.

Hurry towards the gate,
for here you shall not stay. *(Let*
them depart out of Paradise, with Adam
and Eve following them)
Your digging tools
and your things for spinning
are ready.

Let them put on the garments
and show a spade and a distaff.

Death

Me yw cannas Dew, Ankow,
Omma dretha appoyntys.
Rag terry gormenadowe
Tha Adam gans Dew ornys,
Ef a verve, hay ayshew.

Yn della ythew poyntyes
Tha vyns a vewa in byes
Me the latha gans ow gew.

Adam na Eva pegha
Ha deffan an Tas terry,
Mernans ny wressans tastya
Mes in pleasure venarye
Y a wressa prest bewa.

Omma eve ytho poyntyes
Chief warden war Paradice,
Ha der pegh a Coveytes
Oll y joye ythew kellys,
May fetha paynes ragtha.

Gans an Jowle yfowns tulles
Der an Serpent malegas,
Dell welsowgh warbarth omma.

Deathe departeth awaye.

Adam

Henna ythew trewath bras,
Ny tha vonas mar gucky
May thew kellys thyn an place
O ornes thyn, lean a joye,
Tha vewa omma neffra.

1004 sd. *at 1001 in MS.*
1005. *1003 repeated in MS after this line.*

[Death comes forward.]

Death

I am Death, God's messenger,
appointed by him here.
For breaking the commandment
ordained to Adam by God,
he and his issue will die.

Thus it is appointed
to all who shall live in the world
that I shall kill them with my dart.

Had Adam and Eve not sinned
and broken the Father's command,
they would not have tasted death,
but they would live for ever
in eternal pleasure.

Here he was appointed
chief warden over Paradise,
and through the sin of Covetousness
all his joy is lost,
that he shall have punishment for it.

They were deceived by the Devil
through the cursed Serpent,
as you have seen together here.

Death goes away.

Adam

That is great sadness,
that we were so foolish
that the place is lost to us
that was ordained for us, full of joy,
to live here eternally.

Lemyn, Eva ow fryas,
Henna ytho tha folly gye.
Rag henna paynes pur vras
Yma ornes ragan ny,
May hellyn kyny dretha.

Eva Me ny wothyan gwyll dotha,
Kemmys gyrryow teake am beff.
Der henna, war ow ena,
Me a supposyas eall Neffe
Y thova denvenys thym.

Sera, kenfoma cregys,
Y flattering o mar gloryes
Ny wothyan guthell nahean
Rom lea lowta.

Adam A, soweth te tha gregye
Than Jowle bras hay anfugye!
Rag ytho ef re wylly
Pen eth in Serpent agye
Rag tha dulla.

A ban omma cowle dyckles, 12r
Haga Paradice hellys,
Me a vyn dallath palas

Rag cawas susten ha boos
Thymo ve ha thom flehys,
Hag aparell a thyllas.

Eva Yn weth me a vyn netha,
Rag gule dillas thom cutha
Ha thom flehys es genys.

Now, Eve my wife,
that was your folly.
Because of that great punishment
is set aside for us,
and we may lament it.

Eve I did not know how to deal with him,
I received so many fair words.
Because of that, on my soul,
I believed he was an angel of Heaven
sent to me.

Sir, even if I were to be hanged,
his persuasive words were so delightful
I did not know how to act otherwise,
on my true honour.

Adam Oh, alas that you believed
the great Devil and his deceits!
For he was too cunning
when he entered the Serpent
to trick you.

Since I am quite homeless,
and driven from Paradise,
I will begin to dig

to obtain livelihood and food
for me and for my children,
and material for clothing.

Eve I will spin too,
to make clothes to cover myself
and for my children who have been born.

Adam Ethlays, gwef pan veve genys,
Ow terry gormenadow Dew!
Hellys one a Paradice
Than noer veys, er agen gew.
Tra vetholl a rella leas
Ny gavaf omma neb tew,
Na susten, moy es bestas.
Fatla wren omwetha bew?

Eva Nynsew helma Paradice,
Anagew, Adam, nagew!
Ena y thesa flowrys
Ha frutes, teke aga lew,
    Thagan maga,

Orta meras pan wrellan.
Channgys yw an rowle lemyn.
    Ellas orthan pref cola!

Adam Deaw vabe yma thym genys,
Ha tevys y thyns tha dues.
    Why oll as gweall.
    Shew hes two sonnes.
Cayne ythew ow mabe cotha,
Ha Abell ew ow mabe yoncka,
    Flehys evall ha gentill.

(he speakethe to Cayne) Me a vyn
  thewhy poyntya
Service tha chardg hay gela,
    Rag rowlya eys ha chattell.

1039. gormenadow *Stokes;* gormenadew *MS.*
1040. Hellys *Stokes;* Gellys *MS.*
1059. gentill gentll *MS.*
1061. chardg *this ed;* teag *MS;.*

Adam

Alas, woe is me that I was born,
breaking God's commandment!
We are driven from Paradise
into the world, to our grief.
Nothing at all that might prove of profit
do I find anywhere here,
nor food, other than animals.
How shall we keep ourselves alive?

Eve

This is not Paradise,
ah, it is not, Adam, it is not!
There there were flowers,
and fruit, beautiful in colour,
to feed us,

whenever we might look at them.
The regime has changed now.
Alas that I listened to the snake!

Adam

Two sons are born to me,
and they are grown into men.
You all see them.
Show his two sons.
Cain is my elder son,
and Abel is my younger son:
modest and well-behaved children.

(he speaks to Cain) I shall
appoint you both
service to one job and the other,
to control corn and cattle.

Cayne, tha chardg ge a vythe
War kerth, barlys, ha gwanethe,
    Tha wethill an dega leall.

(he turneth to Abell) Hag Abell, an oblashyon
War an beastas han nohan,
    Han devidgyow oll in gweall.

Ha penvo reys degevy
Gorowgh y than Mownt Tabor,
Hag ena gwrewh aga lyskye,
Dowt Dew genow tha serry
    Mar ny wreen oblacion leall.

Cayme Adam ow thas caradowe,
Me ara heb falladowe
    Tha worhemmyn yn tean.

Reys yw, purryes lavyrrya
Ha gones an beise omma -
    Tha gawas theny susten.

A lamb redy, with fyre and insence.

Abell Mos then menythe me a vyn
Ha gwyll an dega lemyn,
    Ha lesky holma pur glane.

Han degvas oll a bub tra, 12v
Oblasshion sure anotha,
    Mean dylla oll gans tane.

1072. tha *Stokes;* that *MS.*
1079 sd. *at 1074 in MS.*

Cain, your charge shall be
over oats, barley and wheat,
to make the true tithe.

(he turns to Abel) And Abel, the offering
over the animals and the oxen,
and all the sheep in the field.

And when it is needful to tithe,
take them to Mount Tabor,
and burn them there,
lest God be angry with you
if we do not make a true offering.

Cain

My dear father Adam,
without fail I will carry out
your orders to the letter.

It is essential, most essential to toil
and till the ground here -
[*aside*] to get ourselves food.

A lamb ready, with fire and incense.

Abel

I shall go to the mountain
and make the tithe now,
and burn all this to the bare bone.

And the whole tenth part of it all,
an offering from it indeed,
I shall dispatch fully with fire.

Cayme Ye lysky ny vannaf ve,
An eys nan frutes defrye.
Taw, Abell, thymo, pedn cooge!

Me a guntell dryne ha spearn
Ha glose tha leskye heb bearn,
Hag ara bush brase a vooge.

Abell Cayne, nyngew henna gwryes vas.
Yn gorthyans tha Thew an Tase,
Gwren agen sacrafice leall.

Dew a therfyn bos gwerthyes
Gans an gwella frute pub preys.
Me an gwra, aus merwall.

Cayne, ow brodar,
Mere ha predar:
Hemma yw moog wheake.

Cayme Taw, theth cregye!
Hema yw gwell defry,
Te foole crothacke.

Abell Ny yll bos,
Pan wreth gans glos
Thethe sacrafice.

Cayme Re Thew an rose,
Mensan tha vos
Ughall cregys!
A chawbone readye.
Rag errya, sure, war ow fyn,
Me athe wiske, harlott jawdyn,
May thomelly theth kylban!

Cain

Burn it I shall not,
the corn nor the fruits indeed.
Be quiet, Abel, dimwit!

I'll collect thorns and briars
and cowpats to burn without regret,
and will make a huge bush of smoke.

Abel

Cain, that is not well done.
In honour of God the Father,
let us make our sacrifice faithfully.

God deserves to be worshipped
with the best fruit always.
I shall do it, even if I die.

Cain, my brother.
look, and consider:
this is sweet smoke.

Cain

Hang you, be quiet!
Of course this is better,
you fat-bellied fool.

Abel

It can't be,
when you make
your sacrifice with cowpats.

Cain

By God who made me, [*God descends and watches from behind*]
I wish you were
hanged high!
A jawbone ready.
For grumbling at me, surely,
I shall beat you, you villain,
that you fall on the back of your head.

Kymar henna,
Te ploos adla,
Waran challa gans askern an challa!

Abell ys stryken with a chawebone, and dyeth.

Abell

A trew, aylace!
Te rom lathas,
Cayne, ow brodar.

Yn bysma rag tha wreans
Ty a berth sure gossythyans:
Ken na bredar.

Cayne

Otta marow, horssen chorle!
Ny vannaf bos controllys.
He is now ryd owt of the world.
Y fensan y voos cuthys
In neb toll kea.

An gwase a vynsa leskye
Agen esowe, in tevery.
Ny yllan perthy henna.

Tha Thew nyngeis otham vythe
A woos cawas agen pythe,
Me a wore gwyre.

Ow thase, kenfova serrys
Pan glowa an nowethys
Y vos lethys, me, ew heare,
Ny sensaf poynt.

Take that,
you dirty outcast,
on the jaw with a jawbone!

Abel is struck with a jawbone and dies.

Abel

O woe, alas!
You have killed me,
Cain, my brother.

You will certainly suffer punishment
in this world for your doing:
don't think otherwise.

Cain

Look, he's dead, poor bastard!
I won't be ordered about.
He's now rid out of the world.
I wish he were hidden
in some hedge-hole.

The fellow would have burnt
our corn, indeed.
I couldn't put up with that.

God has no need at all
to take our property,
I know truly.

Although my father may be angry
when he hears the news
that he is killed, I, who am heir,
shan't mind a bit.

Cast Abell into a dyche.
Merowgh pymava towles,
In cleath tha vonas peddrys!
Nymbes yddrag vyth in beise,
Owe doarn kethewa lethys,
Pare deloma gwicker coynt.

Father *(When the Father speakethe to Cayme, lett hem looke downe)* Cayme, thyma, pyma Abell?
Ow gweryby uskys gwra.

Cayne Ny won, Arluthe, dyhogall; 13r
Henna te a wore ynta.

My nyngof warden thotha.
Perhape blygh, so mot I go,
An lathas pols a lema
An harlot ploos.

Cooth ew eve hag avlethis,
Panna ylla omweras?
Y vaw ny vidnan boos.

Father Yta voice mernans Abell
Thethe vrodar, prest ow kylwall
An doer warnas pub tellar.

Malegas nefra reby;
Hag oll an tyer a bewfy
Ew malegas yth ober.

Frute da bydnar re thocka,
Na dadar arall neb preise.
Ow molath yrof thyʒa;
Molath ow Mabe haw Sperys
Thyso kymmar.

1157. bewfy *Nance;* bewhy *MS.*

Throw Abel into a ditch.

See where he is thrown,
into a ditch to rot!
I have no repentence in the world whatsoever,
though he was killed by my hand,
artful dealer that I am.

[*God approaches.*]

Father — *(When the Father speaks to Cain, let him look down)* Cain, where is Abel?
Answer me quickly.

Cain — I don't know, Lord, I'm sure;
that you know well.

I am not his keeper.
As I may live, perhaps a wolf
has killed him some way away,
the dirty rascal.

Is he old and wretched,
since he can't look after himself?
I wouldn't be his servant.

[*A voice cries out.*]

Father — Behold the voice of the death of Abel
your brother, calling always
upon you everywhere from the earth.

May you ever be cursed;
and all the land that you own
is cursed by your deed.

May it never bear good fruit,
nor ever other goodness.
My curse I give to you;
the curse of my Son and my Spirit
take unto you.

Cayme *(Let not Cayme looke in the Fatheris face, but look down and quake)* Theth
voyce, Arluth, a glowaf,
Saw tha face me ny wellaf,
Sure er ow gew.

Moy ew ow gwan oberowe
Hag in wethe ow fehosowe
Es tell ew tha vercy, Dew,
Thym tha ava.

Lemyn deffryth ove ha gwag,
Pur wyre drees oll tues an byes.
Me ny won leverall praga
Gans peb na vethaf lethys
En rage an keth obarma.

Father Cayme, na vethys indella.
Rag tha latha dean mar qwra
Eve an gevyth seyth kemmys.

Token warnas me a wra. *(Let the Father make a marcke in his forehedd; this worde: Omega)*
Henna gwelys pan vova
Ny vethis gans dean towches.

Cayme Me a vyn mose thom sera,
Tha welas pana fara
A wra ef an nowethys.

Now God speda theis, ow thase.
Me a wrug oblashion brase,
Hag a loskas shower a yees.

Cain *(Let Cain not look into the Father's face, but look down and quake)* Lord,
I hear your voice,
but your face I do not see,
surely to my great grief.

Greater is my wrong-doing
and my sins also
than is your mercy, God,
to forgive me.

Now I am wretched and empty
most truly beyond all men in the world.
I cannot tell why
I shall not be killed by all
even for this very deed.

Father Cain, you shall not be so.
For if a man do kill you
he shall have it back seven fold.

I shall make a sign upon you. *(Let the Father make a mark on his forehead; this word: Omega)*
When that is seen
you will not be touched by a man.

Cain I will go to my father,
to see what notice
he will take of the news.
[Cain goes to Adam.]
Now God speed you, my father.
I have made a great offering,
and have burnt a deluge of corn.

Adam

Henna ytho gwryes pur tha.
Pyma Abell, cowes henna:
Der nagewa devethys?

The Father depart to Heaven.

Cayme

Anotha marsses predar,
Worth y wothyas govena...
A rogella ye vrodar.
Me an syns gwethe es bucka;
Ny won py theth tha wandra.

Adam

Hemma ythew gorryb skave; 13v
Yma ow gwyll ow holan clave
Wartha glowas in tornma.

Ty ren lathas, rom lowta!
Ow molath theis rag henna,
Ha molath tha vabm ganso
Te a vith sure magata.
An nowothow pan glowa
Y holan terry a wra.
Omskemynes del ota,
Quicke in ker ke a lebma,
Ny berraf gweall ahanas,

Rag cavow sevall om saf.
War doer lemyn omhelaf.
Ow holan ter deaw gallas.

Cayne

Omskemnys lower y thove,
Nyngew reis skemyna moye.
Nyth anea, perth ge cove,
Na ow dama, in teffrye.
Me a vyn kyns es hethy
Mos a lema,

Adam

That was very well done.
Where is Abel, tell me that:
has he really not come?

The Father depart to Heaven.

Cain

If you're concerned about him
ask his keeper...
[*aside*] if his brother's hidden him.
I think him worse than a hobgoblin;
I don't know where he's gone
wandering.

Adam

This is a flippant reply;
it is making my heart sick
to listen to you now.

You have killed him, by my troth!
My curse upon you for it,
and you will surely have with it
the curse of your mother too.
When she hears the news
her heart will break.
Get away from here quickly,
cursed as you are.
I cannot bear the sight of you,

nor stand upright for sorrow.
I shall cast myself now on the ground.
[*falls down*]
My heart has gone in two.

Cain

I am cursed enough,
there is no need to curse any more.
I shall not trouble you, remember,
nor my mother, indeed.
I shall immediately
go away,

Ha gwandra adro in powe.
Kebmys yw an molothowe
Dowt yw thym cawas trygva.

Eva *(Eva commeth to Adam wher he lyeth, and she profer to take hem upe)*

Adam, pandra whear thewhy,
Yn delma bonas serrys?
Un ow holan pur thefry
Ythoma pur dewhan hees
Ortha welas in statema.

Adam

A, Eva, ow freas kear,
Ow holan ew ogas troghe.
Oll owe joye ythew pur wyre
Kellys, der mernans ow floghe
Neb a geryn an moygha.

Eva

Sera, ny won convethas
Ages dewan in neb for.
Agen deaw vabe, ȝa Thew grace,
Ythyns pur vew - byth na sor -
Whath nyngew pell.

Cayme hag Abell, te a wore,
Ornys yns tha Vownt Tabor
Tha weyll offren, dehogall.

Ha meer, Cayne yta ena,
Devethys tha dre tothta.
Rag henna saf, y praytha,
Ha gas cavow ȝa wandra.
Me ne brederaf gwell for.

1220 sd. *so placed in Nance; at 1216 in MS.*

and wander about in the land.
The curses are so many
that I doubt I shall find a home.

Eve

(Eve comes to where Adam lies,
and she should attempt to lift him up)
What is your sorrow, Adam,
that you are troubled so?
I am very unhappy
indeed in my heart
at seeing you in this state.

Adam

Ah, Eve, my dear wife,
my heart is almost broken.
Truly all my joy is
lost, through the death of my child
whom I loved the most.

Eve

Sir, I cannot understand
your grief at all.
Our two sons, thank God,
were alive and well - do not grieve -
not long since.

You know Cain and Abel
have been ordered to Mount Tabor
to make an offering, in truth.

And look, there is Cain,
quickly come home.
So stand up, I beg you,
and let sorrows wander.
I cannot think of a better way.

Adam Eva, nyngew tha gellas
An obar ma tha wellas.
Lethys yw Abell. Na sor.

Eva *(Eva is sorowfull, tereth her heare, and falleth downe upon Adam. He conforteth her)* Pewa! Abell yw lethys! 14r
Dew defan y foʒa gwyre!
Nynges dean vytholl in byes
Tha wythell an kethe murder,
Mes te haw mabe cotha Cayne.

Adam A, gans Cayme omskemynes
Ow mabe Abell yw lethys,
May thove genys tha veare bayne.

Sor Dew ha trobell pub tew
Yma pub ower ow cressya.
Yn bysma ha drevon bew
Ow sure a wra penya.
Nymbef joy a dra in byes.

Eva Owt, aylas, pandra byth gwryes?
Hemma ew yeyne nawothowe.
Ow holan ythew terrys;
Fensan ow bosaf marowe.
Soweth bythqwathe bos formys!

A, te Cayme omskemunys,
Ow molath theʒo pub preys!
Henna o gwan obar gwryes,
May ma Dew han noer keffrys
Warnas pub ere ow crya.

1246 sd. *at 1243 in MS.*
1254. trobell trobll *MS.*

Adam

Eve, there is no hiding
this deed from being seen.
Abel is killed. Do not grieve.

Eve

*(Eve is sorrowful, tears her hair,
and falls down upon Adam. He
comforts her)* What! Abel is killed!
God forbid it should be true!
There is no man in the world
to commit that murder,
except you and my elder son Cain.

Adam

O, by cursed Cain
my son Abel has been killed,
and I am born to great pain.

The wrath of God and trouble everywhere
are increasing every hour.
As long as I live in this world
He will surely punish me.
I have no joy of anything in the world.

Eve

O, alas, what is to be done?
This is chill news.
My heart is broken;
I wish I were dead.
Alas that ever I was made!

Ah, you damned Cain,
my curse on you for ever!
That was a bad deed done,
and God and the earth too are
crying out on you continually.

Rag henna, woȝa hemma,
Nefra ny wren rejoycya,
Mes pub ere oll ow mornya
Heb joy vyth na lowena
    Der tha wadn ober omma.

Rag henna voyde a lema,
Na whela agen nea,
    Mab molothow pardel os.

Ow molath theȝo pub preys,
Ha molath tha dase keffrys
    Te a vyth in gyth ha noos.

Cayne

Me ny wraf vry a henna,
Me a levar theis dama.
Kybmys mollothow omma,
Me a wore ny sewenaffa
    Nefra yn beyse.

Rag henna mos a lemma
Me a vyn; ny won pylea.
Malbew yddrag es thyma
An chorle Abell us latha,
    Rag bythqwath me nyn kerys.
    (Cayme speakethe to hys wiff)
                A voyd, dama.

Cuntell warbarth ow fegans:
Me a vyn mos pur uskys
Ha woȝa hemma dewhans,
Pell in devythe tha wandra.

1289. *this ed; follows 1286 in MS.*
1290 sd. *at 1285 in MS.*

Therefore, after this,
we shall never rejoice,
but for ever all be mourning,
without any joy or gladness,
because of your bad deed here.

So go away,
do not try to trouble us,
son of curses as you are.

My curse upon you always,
and the curse of your father too
you will have day and night.

Cain I don't care about that,
I tell you, mother.
Here are so many curses,
I know I shall not prosper
ever in the world.

So I'll go away;
I don't know where.
I haven't a damn bit of repentance
for killing the wretch Abel,
for I never loved him.
(Cain speaks to his wife)
Come away, woman.

Get my things together:
I shall go hastily
and directly after this
to wander far into the wilderness.

Calmana his wif

A, Cayne, Cayme, ow fryas kere,
Ty a wruge pur throog ober
    Tha latha Abell, dean da.

Theth owne vrodar ythova, 14v
Haw brodar ve magata.
Rag henna warbyn cunda
Y tho theis motty latha.
    Sor Dew yma thyn ragtha.

Cayne

Tety valy, bram an gathe!
Nynges yddrag thymo whath
    A wos an keth ober na.

Adam

Ow fryas, gwella tha geare:
Gas tha ola hath ega.
Gwren grasse thagen maker
Agan lavyr in bysma;
    Ny andyllas, ha moye.

Rag henna, woȝa hemma,
In chast gwren ny kes vewa;
Ha carnall joye in bysma
Ny a vyn warbarthe naha,
    Der vothe an Tase a vercye.

Father

Adam, na wrethe in della
Bewa in kethe order na.
Theth hays a wra incressya
Heb nunnber tha accomptya,
    In della ythew apoyntyes.

Ty a vyth mabe denethys
Athe corf sure, nawra dowtya.
Henna a vyth havall theis
(Na yll dean bos havalla),
    Ha genaf yfyth kerrys.

Calmana his wife

Ah, Cain, Cain, my dear husband,
you have done a very evil deed
in killing Abel, a good man.

He was your own brother,
and my brother too.
Therefore it was against nature
for you to go and kill him.
We have God's anger for it.

Cain

Tety valy, the cat's fart!
I have no repentance yet
for that same deed.

Adam

Cheer yourself, my wife:
stop your weeping and wailing.
Let us thank our maker
for our trouble in this world;
we have deserved it, and more.

Therefore, from now on,
let us live together chastely;
and we will together forswear
carnal joy in this world,
through the will of the Father of mercy.

Father

(speaking from Heaven) Adam, you shall not so
live in that condition.
Your seed shall increase
without number to be counted,
so it is appointed.

You will have a son born
surely from your body; do not fear.
He will be like you
(a man cannot be more like)
and he will be loved by me.

Adam — *(Adam kneleth)* Arluth, benegas re by,
Orth ow gwarnya in della.
Theth vlonogath pur theffry
Rebo collenwys neffra.

Cayne — Kalmana ow hoer, fysten,
Gas ny tha vos a lemma,
Rag nangew hy pryes yttean
Mathew res in ker vaggya.
    Degen genan agen pegans,

Pardelosta ow fryas
Haw hoer abarth mam ha tase.
Gallas genaf sor an Tase
Rag latha Abell pen braas;
Yn weth molath mam ha taes
    Reis ew thymo - moy es cans.

Kalmana — A, Cayme, te a fylles mear
Rag gwethell an keth obar;
    Ragtha ythos malegas.

Agen tase ha mam Eva 15r
Lower y mowns y ow murnya.
    Ganssy ny vyth ankevys
    An murder bys venary.

Kebmys ew ganssy murnys
Aga holan ew terrys
    Rag cavow, methaf y dy.

1332. yttean *this ed;* yttern *MS;* ynten *Stokes.*

Adam *(Adam kneels)* Lord, blessed may you be
for so informing me.
May your will most truly
ever be fulfilled.

Cain Hurry, Calmana my sister,
let us go away,
for it is now high time
that we should travel away.
Let us carry our things with us,

as you are my wife,
and my sister by both mother and father.
I have gained the wrath of the Father
for killing bighead Abel;
also the curse of mother and father
has been given to me - more than a hundred.

Calmana Ah, Cain, you have sinned greatly
in commiting that act;
you are cursed for that.

Our father and Eve our mother
are sorrowing greatly.
The murder will never
be forgotten by them.

They have sorrowed so much
their heart is broken
with grief, I dare swear it.

Cayne A wos henna ny wraf wry;
Na anothans y bys voye,
    Me ny settyaf gwaile gala.

Genaf lower y a sorras
Rag an molythys mar vras
    Ny sowynaf, gon ynta,
    Nefra in byes.

Rag henna dune a lema
Yn peldar tha worthe ow thase.
Yn cosow mannaf bewa,
Po in bushes ha brakes brase;
    Rag ny bydgyaf bos gwelys
    A wos mernans.

Rag an murder o mar vrase
Ny yll Dew thymo gava,
Na ny vethaf in neb case
Than Taes, a wos descotha,
    Unwyth tha whelas gevyans.
    Lett hem shew the marck.

Kalmana Yn henna ythos tha vlamya.
Dew a settyas merke warnas,
En in corne tha dale omma,
Ha in delma y leverys,
    An gyrryow ma, pur thefry:

Pynagell dean a weall henna
Haga wrella tha latha,
    Ef astevyth seyth plague moy.

1352. voye *Stokes*; veye *MS*.

Cain

I don't care about that;
I don't set a straw
by them any more.

They have been angry enough with me
and cursed me so greatly
that I shall not prosper, I know well,
ever in the world.

Therefore let us go away
a long distance from my father.
I mean to live in the woods,
or in bushes and great brakes;
for I'm praying not to be seen
in case of death.

For the murder was so great
God can't forgive me,
and in any case I shan't dare
to ask forgiveness once
from the Father, for fear of discovery.

Let him show the mark.

Calmana

In that you are to blame.
God has set a mark on you,
even here in the horn of your forehead,
and thus he spoke,
these very words, most truly:

Whatsoever man sees that
and should kill you,
he will obtain seven plagues more.

Cayme

An promas me ny roof oye;
Y dristya ny vannaf vye
Dowt boos tulles.

A ban ew pub tra parys,
Deen ny in kerth kekeffres,
Peldar a dro in byes.
Som fardell to carie with them.
Hagen flehis kekeffrys:
Whath kethyns y mar venys
Me a thog ran war ow hyen.
Uskes lemyn.

Kalmana

Gwra in della, me ath peys;
Me a lead an voos am dorn.
Ow holan ythew serres,
That sithe the tyme I was borne
Bythqwath my nynbeys moy dewan.

Adam

Gorthys rebo Dew an Tase! 15v
Mabe thymo yma genys,
Ha tevys tha baga brase.
Seth ow mabe ythew henwys;
Why an gweall: yta omma.
Shew Seth.
Me abyes than leall Drenges
Ha drevo omma in beys
Tha voes leall servant thoȝo.

Father

Adam, me a levar theys
Tha vabe Seth ew đowesys
Genaf prest thom servya ve.

1394. tha baga *this ed;* that Baga *MS.*

Cain

I don't give an egg for the promise;
I shan't trust it
for fear of being tricked.

Since everything is ready,
let us go away too,
far off somewhere in the world.
Some bundle to carry with them.
And our children too:
since they are still so small
I'll carry one on my back.
Quickly now.

Calmana

Please do so;
I'll lead the girl by my hand.
My heart is troubled,
that since the time I was born
I have never felt greater grief.

[*Exit Cain with his family.*]

Adam

Glory be to God the Father!
A son has been born to me,
and grown to a big boy.
He is called Seth, my son;
you see him: here he is.
Show Seth
I pray to the true Trinity
that as long as he is here in the world
he may be a faithful servant to Him.

Father

Adam, I say to you
that your son Seth has been chosen
by me to serve me always.

A skeans yfyth lenwys,
Hag a gonnycke magata.
Ny vyth seans vyth in beys
Mes y aswon ev a wra
    Der an planantys, meas ha chy.

Der howle ha steare a wartha
Ef ara oll desernya
An pyth a vyth woȝa hemma,
    Kekefrys a throg ha da.

Adam *(Adam kneleth, and Seth also)*
Mear worthyans theis, ow formyour,
Ha gwrear a oll an beyse.
Y bosta Arluth heb pare;
In pub place rebo gwerthys.
Neb ath honor ny throg fare.
Yn Seth rebo collenwys
    Pare delvo tha voth nefra
    Omma pur greyf.

Seth Ha me in weth, Arluth Neif,
Ath leall wones delvo reys,
Pardell osta Arluth creif,
Ha drevon omma yn byes.
    Clow ge ow leaf,

Mayne bone grace woȝa hemma
Theth welas in lowendar,
Gans tha elath a wartha
    Uhall in Neyf.

1412 sd. *at 1414 in MS.*

He will be filled with knowledge,
and with skill as well.
There will be no learning in the world
that he will not know
inside out, by means of the planets.

Through the sun and the stars above
he will understand all
of the things that shall be after this,
both of good and evil.

Adam *(Adam kneels, and Seth also)*
Great honour to you, my creator,
and maker of all of the world.
You are Lord without equal;
may he be worshipped everywhere.
He who honours you will not go wrong.
In Seth may it be fulfilled
according to your will always
here most forcefully.

Seth And I also, Lord of Heaven,
shall serve you loyally as I should,
mighty Lord as you are,
as long as I am here in the world.
Hear my voice,

that we may have grace after this
to see you in joy,
with your angels above
high in Heaven.

Lamec in tent

Peys! Golsowogh, a der dro,
Orthaf ve myns es omma.
Lamec ythew ow hanowe;
Mabe ythove, cresowgh thyma,
    Tha Vantusale, forsoth.

A Cayme, mabe Adam ythove
Sevys an sythvas degre.
Arluth bras sengys, in prof.
Nymbes par, suer, ew bewe;
    Peb an honor pardell goyth.

Drog polat ove, rom lowta; 16r
Na mere a dorn da ny wraf,
Mes pub eare oll ow pela
An dues wan mar a callaf.
    Ow fancy yw henna.

Whath kenthew ow hendas Cayne
Pur bad dean lower accomptys,
Me an kymmar in dysdayne
Mar ny vethaf ve prevys
    Whath mere lacka.

Moye es un wreag thym yma
Thom pleasure rag gwyll ganssy.
Ha sure me ew an kensa
    Bythqwath whath a ve dew wreag.

Han mowyssye lower plenty
Yma thym; nyngens dentye.
Me as kyef pan vydnaf ve;
Ny sparyaf anothans y,
    Malbew onyn a vo teag.

Lamech in tent

Quiet! Listen
to me, everyone who is here.
Lamech is my name; [*he emerges*]
I am son, believe me,
to Methusael, forsooth.

From Cain, the son of Adam, I am
descended, in the seventh degree.
Considered to be a great lord, obviously.
I have no equal that's alive, surely;
all honour me as they ought.

I'm a bad fellow, on my honour;
I don't do many good turns,
but I'm always bullying
the weak people if I can.
That's my fancy.

Even though my forefather Cain is
considered a thoroughly bad man,
I shall be most scornful
if I am not proved
much worse still.

I have more than one wife
to take my pleasure with.
And surely I'm the first
ever yet to have two wives.

And I have young ladies in plenty;
they aren't choosy.
I have them whenever I like;
I never keep away from them,
damnwell not from one that's pretty.

Saw ythove wondrys trobles;
Skant ny welaf un banna.
Pew an jowle! Pandra vyth gwryes?
Me ny won, war owe ena,
    Na whath ny gavaf gweras.

An pleasure es thym in beyse
Ythew gans gwaracke tedna.
Me a vyn mos pur uskes
Than forast quyck a lema,
    Ha latha an strange bestas.

A us kyek an bestas na,
Na a veast na lodn in beyse
Ny wressan bythqwath tastya.
Na whath kyk genyn debbrys,
    Na gwyne ny usyan badna.

Vyctuall erall theyn yma,
Ha pegans lower tha vewa.
Gans krehen an bestas na
My ara dyllas thyma,
    Par delwrug ow hendasow.

Haw hendas Cayme, whath ew bew
Yn defyth; in myske bestas
    Yma ef prest ow pewa.

Drevan serry an Taes Dew
Towles ew tha vyshew bras,
    Rag drog polat pardell ew
    Ha lenwys a volothowe.

1459. banna ba$\overline{nn}$a *MS*.

But I'm strangely troubled;
I can hardly see a bit.
What the devil! What's to be done?
I don't know, upon my soul,
and I haven't found any cure yet.

The one pleasure that I have in the world
is to shoot with a bow.
I shall go very hastily
away to the forest quickly,
and kill the wild beasts.

Hitherto we have never yet tasted
the flesh of those beasts,
or of any animal or beast in the world.
Flesh has not yet been eaten by us,
nor do we use wine at all.

We have other victuals,
and enough things to live.
I shall make clothes for myself
from the skins of those beasts
as my ancestors did.

And my ancestor Cain, he still lives
in the desert; among the beasts
he's living permanently.

Because he angered God the Father
he is cast into great trouble,
like the bad fellow that he is
and full of curses.

Bowe and arrow redy with the servant. 16v

Ow servant, des nes omma,
Haw gwaracke dro hy genas.
Me a vyn mos tha wandra
Bestas gwylls tha asspea,
    Hag a vyn gans ow sethaw
    Latha part anothans y.

Depart Lameck. His servant leadethe hem to the forest, near the bushe.

Servant Ages gweracke ha sethow
Genaf y towns y parys.
Me as lead bezyn cosow,
Hag ena yfythe kevys
    Plenty lower, in pur thefry.

Cayne Gans peb me ew ankevys;
Nyn aswon na mere a dues.
Cayne me a vyth henwys,
Mabe cotha Adam, towles,
    Why a weall, tha vysshew bras.

Whath ow holan ythew stowte
A wos latha Abell lowte,
    Na whath, us molathe an Tase,
    Nymbes yddrack vyth in beys.

Why am gweall: over devys
Y thoma warbarthe gans bleaw.
Ny bydgyaf bonas gwelys
Gans mabe den in bysma bew,
    Drefan om boos omskemynes.

1485 sd. *arrow* Arr *MS.*
1488. asspea *(Nance)*; asspeas *MS.*

Bow and arrow ready with the servant.

Come here, my servant,
and bring my bow with you.
I shall go wandering
to look for wild beasts,
and with my arrows I shall
kill some of them.

Lamech depart. His servant leads him to the forest, near the bush.

Servant

Look, I have ready
your bow and arrows.
I'll take you right to the woods,
and there will be found
plenty enough, indeed.

[*The forest.*]

Cain

I am forgotten by everyone;
not many people recognise me.
Cain is my name,
Adam's elder son, fallen,
as you see, into great trouble.

My heart is still bold
on account of killing the lout Abel,
nor do I have any repentance at all
yet, in spite of the curse of the Father.

You see me: I am overgrown
completely with hair.
I cannot bear to be seen
by any man living in the world,
because of my being cursed.

Haw thas Adam y volath
Gallas genaf, hay sor braes.
Drefan henna, in neb place
Ny allaf gawas powas;
Mabe molothow yʒof gwryes.

Der henna my ny vethaf
Doos in myske pobell neb pryes,
Mes pub ere ow omgwetha
Yn cossowe hag in busshes,
Avell beast prest ow pewa.

Ow folly y thew mar vras,
Haw holan in weth pur browt;
Ny vanaf tha worth an Tase
Whylas mercy, sure heb dowte,
Kynnamboma lowena.

Owne yma thym a bub dean,
Gansa tha vonas lethys.
Saw an Tase Dew y honyn
Y varck warnaf y settyas,
Poran gans y owne dewla.
Why oll an gweall.
Shew the marcke.
Hag yth cowses in delma:
Na wra dean vyth ow latha,
Warbyn y thysplesure leell.

Hag owe latha neb a wra, 17r
Seyth gwythe y wra acquyttya,
Y cowses, gans chardg pur greyf.

Saw whath, wos an promes na,
Meare y thesaf ow towtya
Y bedna ʒym ny vyn ef.

I have received both the curse
of my father Adam,
and his great anger.
Because of that, nowhere
can I find rest;
I am made a son of curses.

Therefore I do not dare
to come among people at any time,
but always hide myself
in woods and in bushes,
constantly living like a beast.

My folly is so great,
and also my heart very proud;
I won't seek mercy from the Father,
that's certain,
although I'm unhappy.

I'm afraid of every man,
that I should be killed by him.
But God the Father himself
set his mark upon me,
with his very own hands.
You all see it.
Show the mark.

And thus he spoke:
that no man at all shall kill me,
on peril of his righteous indignation.

And he that shall kill me,
he will pay it back sevenfold,
he said, with a most strict injunction.

But yet, in spite of that promise,
I am very much afraid
he won't give me his blessing.

Rag henna, war ow ena,
Me a vyn mos tha gutha
In neb bushe, kythew thym greyf.
Let hem hyd hem self in a bushe.

Servant
Mester da, der tha gymmyas -
Me a weall un lodn pur vras
Hans in bushe ow plattya.

Sera, in myske an bestas
Strange ythew eve tha welas.
Merowgh, mester, pymava.

Lamec
Bythware thym navova dean,
Rag me ny allaf meddra.
Set ow seth the denewhan,
May hallan tenna thotha.
Na berth dowt, y fythe gwyskes.

Let his man levyll the arrowe; and then shote.

Servant
Neffra na wrewgh why dowtya,
Ken es beast nagew henna,
Ha strange yw tha vos gwelys.

Now yta an seath compys;
Tenhy in ban besyn peyll,
Pardell os archer prevys
Hag a lathas moy es myell
A vestas kyns es lemyn.

Lamec
Now yta an seth tennys,
Han beast sure yma gweskes!
Y vernans gallas gonȝa!

When Cayme is stryken, lett bloud appeare, and let hem tomble.

Therefore, upon my soul,
I'll go and hide
in some bush, though it upsets me.

Let him hide himself in a bush.

[Lamech approaches, led by his servant.]

Servant

Excuse me, good master --
I see a very large animal
squatting yonder in a bush.

Sir, he's strange to see
among the beasts.
See where he is, master.

Lamech

Take care that it isn't a man,
for I'm not able to aim.
Set my arrow sideways
so that I may shoot at it.
It will be hit, don't worry.

Let his man level the arrow, and then shoot.

Servant

Don't you never fear,
that isn't nothing but a beast,
and strange it is to be seen.

Now see the arrow level;
draw it up as far as the head,
as you are an experienced archer
and have killed more than a thousand
beasts before now.

Lamech

Now see the arrow shot,
and the beast is surely hit!
Its death has come upon it!

When Cain is struck, let blood appear, and let him tumble.

Lead ve quycke besyn thotha,
May hallan ve attendya
Pan vanar lon ythewa.

Cayne

Owt, aylas, me yw marowe!
Nymbes bewa na fella!
Gwenys ove der an assow,
Han segh gallas quyte drethaf.
Pur ogas marow ythof!

Lamec cometh to hem and fylethe hem.

Pardell vema ungrasshes,
Lemyn y thoma plagys,
Dell welowgh why oll an prove.

Lamec

Owt, te vyllan, pandres gwryes?
Sure hema ew dean lethys;
Mean clow prest ow carma.

Servant

Ow karma yma an beast!
Me an gweall ow trebytchya.
Gallas gonȝa hager feast!
Roy y grohan thym, I praytha,
Tha wyell qweth thym tha wyska.

Blewake coynt yw ha hager; 17v
Ny won pana veast ylla boos.
Yth falsa orth y favoure
Y bosa neb bucka noos,
Ha henna yfyth prevys.

Lead me up to it quickly,
so that I can consider
what sort of animal it is.

Cain O, alas, I'm dead!
I have no longer to live!
I'm pierced through the ribs,
and the arrow has gone right through me.
I'm very nearly dead!

Lamech comes to him and feels him.

Even as I was graceless,
now I am plagued
as you all see the proof.

Lamech [*to his servant*] O, you villain, what's been done?
this is definitely a man killed;
I hear him crying out all the time.

Servant The beast is crying out!
I see him tumbling about.
It has had a bad time!
Give his skin to me, please,
to make an outfit for me to wear.

He's oddly furry and ugly;
I don't know what kind of beast he can be.
It would seem from his appearance
that he's some hobgoblin,
and that will be proved right.

Lamec

Gorta, gas vy the dava,
Drefan gwelas mar nebas. *(Hear Lamec feleth hem)*
Pew osta lavar thymma:
Marses den po neb beast bras.
    Dowt a hanas thym yma.

Cayne

A soweth, umskemynes,
Me ew Cayne, mabe tha Adam.
Genas y thoma lethys.
Molath theis tha das ha mam,
    Haw molath ve gans henna.

Lamec

Pewa! Te ew Cayne, mab tha Adam!
Ny allaf cregye henna.
Defalebys os ha cabm,
Overdevys oll gans henna
    Ythos, gans bleaw.

Prag y thesta in delma
Yn busshes ow crowetha?
    Marth bras ythew.

Me ny allaf convethas
Y bosta ge ow hendas,
    Na care vyth thym, in teffry.

Cayne

Am corf ythos devethys,
Hag a Adam tha hendas.
Lemyn ythose melagas,
Ha seyth plag te hath flehys
    A vyth plagys, creys ȝa ve.

Lamech

Wait, let me feel him,
since I can hardly see. *(Here Lamech feels him)*
[*To Cain*] Tell me who you are:
if you are a man or some great beast.
I am in doubt about you.

Cain

O misery, I am cursed
Cain, son to Adam.
I have been killed by you.
The curse of your father and mother on you,
and my curse with it.

Lamech

What! You are Cain, son to Adam!
I can't believe that.
You're deformed and bent,
all overgrown you are too,
with hair.

Why were you
crouching in the bushes like that?
It's very strange.

I can't believe
that you're my ancestor,
nor any relation of mine, frankly.

Cain

You have come from my body,
and from Adam your forefather.
Now you are cursed,
and with seven plagues you and your children
will be plagued, believe me.

Marcke Dew warnaf ew settys:
Te an gweall in corne ow thale.
Gans dean penvo convethys
Worthaf ve serten ny dale
    Bos mellyes a us neb tra.

Lamec

Te a weall, veary nebas,
Banna ny allaf gwellas
    Tha vos acomptys, rom lowta.

Prag y wruge Dew settya merck
In corn tha dale, thym lavar?
Kyn verhan warnas mar starc
Ny welaf mere ath favoure,
    Na merke vetholl yth tale.

Cayne

Me a levar heb y dye: 18r
Genaf Dew a wrug serry
Hay volath, in pur theffry,
    Thym a rose,

Drefan latha ow brodar.
Abell o henna, predar,
    Mara mynta y wothfas.

Der henna, me a thowtyas
Gans peb y fethan lethys.
Saw Dew thyma a wrontyas -
War y thyspleasure ef ryes -
    Ny vethan in keth della;

Ha penagle a wra henna,
Plages y fetha ragtha.
    Hay verck y settyas omma,
    In corne ow thale, rag token.

The mark of God is set upon me:
you see it in the horn of my forehead.
When a man recognises it
he should certainly not
meddle with me on any account.

Lamech

I can't see a bit,
you see, hardly at all
worth mentioning, by my faith.

Why did God set a mark
on the horn of your forehead, tell me?
Although I'm staring so hard at you
I can't make out much of your appearance,
nor any mark at all on your forehead.

Cain

I'll tell you without putting it on oath:
God became angry with me
and he gave me
his curse, in fact,

for killing my brother.
That was Abel, remember,
since you wish to know.

Because of that, I was afraid
I would be killed by everyone.
But God granted me -
given on peril of his indignation -
that I should not so be;

and whoever does that,
he would be plagued for it.
And he set his mark here,
in the horn of my forehead, as a sign.

Ha genas she, omskemynys,
O me tha vos lethys,
En ath dewlaga lemyn.

Lamec

A, soweth gwelas an pryes
Genaf y bosta lethys,
Marsew ty Cayne ow hendas.

Ow boya o tha vlamya:
Ef a ornas thym tenna,
Ha me, ny wyllyn banna,
Me nebas, pur wyre in faes.

Cayne

A Lamec, drog was y those,
Ha me in weth, mear lacka.
Hemma o vengeance pur vras,
Ha just plage ornys thyma.
Soweth an pryes!

Lamec

Cayne, whath, kenthota ow hendas,
Tha aswon me ny wothyan
(Na ny wrugaf tha wellas
Nangew sure lyas blethan)
Drefan bos defalebys.

Cayne

Defalebys ove pur veare,
Hag over devys gans bleawe.
Bewa y thesaf pub eare
In tomdar ha yender reaw,
Sure nos ha dyth.

Ny bydgyaf gwelas mabe dean
Gans ow both in neb termyn,
Mes company leas gwyth
A bub beastas.

1644. Ha genas *(Nance)*; Ha tha gawas *MS*.

And by you, cursed one,
it was that I am killed,
even now in front of your eyes.

Lamech Oh, alas to see the time
when you are killed by me,
if you are Cain my ancestor.

My boy was to blame:
he ordered me to shoot,
and me, I couldn't see a bit,
me, hardly at all, properly.

Cain Ah Lamech, you are a bad man,
and me too, much worse.
This was a very great vengeance,
and a just punishment ordained for me.
Alas the day!

Lamech Still, Cain, though you are my ancestor,
I didn't know how to recognise you
(I haven't seen you
surely for many years now) -
because you are deformed.

Cain Deformed I certainly am,
and overgrown with hair.
I live always
in heat and frosty cold,
surely day and night.

I can't bear to see a man
at any time by my will,
merely the company many times
of all beasts.

Oll an trobell thym yma
An chorle Abell rag latha.
Hema ew gwyer, thymo trest.

Lameck
Prag ye rusta ye latha,
Hag eve tha vrodar nessa?
Henna o gwadn ober gwryes.

Cayne
Drefan eve thom controllya, 18v
Ha me y vrodar cotha!
Ny wrug refrance thym in beys!

Der henna me a angras
Ha pur uskys an lathas.
Nymbes yddrag a henna.

Molath Dew ha tas ha mam
Gallas genaf ve droag lam
Poran rag an ober na.

Ow holan whath ythew prowte,
Kynthoma ogas marowe.
Mersy whelas y ma thym dowte
Thymo rag an oberow;
Me a wore yvos Dew stowte.
Thymo nyvidn ef gava,
Na gevyans me ny whelaf.

Ye thesaf ow tremena;
Theso ny vannaf gava.
Ow ena ny won pytha:
Tha Effarn ew y drigva.
Ena tregans, gwave ha have.

I have all this trouble
for killing that wretch Abel.
Believe me, this is true.

Lamech Why did you kill him,
and he your closest brother?
That was a bad deed done.

Cain Because of his controlling of me,
and me his elder brother!
He paid no respect to me at all!

So I got angry
and very quickly killed him.
I have no repentance for that.

The curse of God and father and mother
has turned into bad luck for me
just for that act.

My heart is still proud,
although I am nearly dead.
I'm afraid to seek mercy
for myself for the deeds;
I know him to be a firm God.
He will not forgive me,
nor will I look for forgiveness.

I am dying;
I will not forgive you.
My soul is going I know not where:
to Hell that is its home.
Let it stay there, winter and summer.

[*Dies.*]

Lamec

A, soweth gwelas an pryes!
Cayne ow hengyke ew marowe!
Ragtha te a vyth lethys,
A false lader casadowe!
Squattys ew tha apydgnyan!

Kill hem with a staf.

Servant

Owt, aylas, me ew marow,
Haw fedn squatyes pur garow -
Why an gweall - ynter dew ran!

Lamec

Rag henna moes alemma
Me a vydn, gwell a gallaf.
Ny amownt gwythell duwhan
Lemyn ragtha.

Depart away.

First Devyll

Yma Cayne adla marowe.
Deun the hethas tha banowe,
Han pagya Lamec ganso.

Second Devill

Deas, a ena malegas,
Theth vrodar te a lathas
Abell, neb o dean gwyrryan.

Yn tane te a wra lesky,
Han keth pagya ma, defry,
Yn Effarn, why drog lawan.

The devills careth them with great noyes to Hell.

Lamech O, alas to see the time!
Cain my forefather is dead!
You shall be killed for that,
you horrible deceitful thief!
Your brains are shattered!

Kill him with a stick.

Servant O, alas, I'm dead,
with my head savagely shattered -
you see it - into two bits!

Lamech So I shall go away
as best I can.
It's no use making a song and dance
about him now.

Go away.

[Two devils emerge from Hell.]

First Devil That outcast Cain is dead.
Let's go and fetch him to torments,
and Lamech's boy with him.

Second Devil *[to Cain]* Come, you damned soul,
you killed your brother
Abel, who was an honest man.

You're going to burn in fire,
with this boy here, indeed,
in Hell, you malcontents.

The devils carry them with much noise to Hell.

First Devyll

Yn pytt ma y wreth trega
Genaf ve, a bartha wollas,
    Hag a loske in tomdar tane.

Nefra ny thewh a lena,
Myns na wra both an Tas.

Adam

Seth, ow mabe, des omma, 19r
Ha golsow ow daryvas.
Hyrenath bew ove in bysma,
May thove squyth an lavyr bras
    Es thymo pub noos ha dyth.

Rag henna ke a lemma
Tha Baradice heb lettya,
Han Oyle a Vercy whela
Mar kylleth, a us neb tra.
Na thowt, gorryb ty a vyth
    Oll ath negys.

Seyth

A das kear, ny won for thy,
Na nyvef bythqwath ena.
Me ny allaf prederye
Pana gwarton ythama,
    Ser, tha whylas Paradice.

Adam

Gwyth in hans compes tha yest;
Na gymar dowt na mystrust
    Mes an for a vyth kevys
    In vaner ma:

First Devil
You'll stay in this pit
with me, down below,
and burn in the heat of fire.

[*to audience*] You shall never come from there,
all who don't do the will of the Father.

Adam
Come here, Seth, my son,
and hear what I have to say.
I have been alive in this world for a long time,
and I am tired of the hard work
that I have every night and day.

Therefore go from here
to Paradise without delay,
and seek the Oil of Mercy
at all costs, if you can.
Never fear, you will receive an answer
for all your errand.

Seth
O dear father, I do not know the way there,
nor have I ever been there.
I cannot imagine
in which direction I shall go,
sir, to seek Paradise.

Adam
Keep straight to the east yonder;
do not doubt or mistrust
that the path will be found
in this way:

Ty a weall allow ow thryes
Pandeth ve a Baradice;
En an very prynt leskys
Pan ve an noer malegas
    Der ow oberow ena.

Ha pandeffasta than plas,
Ty a gyef in yet udn eall
A ro gorthib theis in case,
Haw desyre nywres fillall.
    Byth avysshes a bub tra
    A welyth, ow mabe, ena.

An Angell in the gate of Paradice: a bright sworde in his hand.

Seyth

Ow thas kere, mos a lema
Me a vyn, en by and by,
Hag y teaf thewhy arta
Gans gorryb, kyns es hethy,
    Der both an Tas a wartha.

Lett Seythe depart and folow the prynt of Adam is feet to Paradice.

Me a weall ooll tryes ow thas,
An lead ve tha Baradice.
Hema ew marrudgyan bras;
An noer sure ny sowenas
    In for may wruge eave kerras.

1750. *Tail-rhyme misplaced after 1745 in MS.*
1766. may *Nance;* my *MS.*

You will see the tracks of my feet
when I came from Paradise;
even the very prints burnt
when the earth was cursed
through my deeds there.

And when you have arrived at the place,
you will find an angel in the gate
who will give you an answer on the matter,
and you will not fail in my wish.
Take note of everything
that you see there, my son.

An Angel in the gate of Paradise,
a bright sword in his hand.

Seth My dear father, I will go away
this very moment,
and return to you again
without delay, with an answer,
through the will of the Father above.

Let Seth depart and follow the
print of Adam's feet to Paradise.

I see the print of my father's foot,
which will lead me to Paradise.
This is a great marvel;
the ground has certainly not
flourished
in the path where he went.

Der temtacion bras an Jowle,
Chasshes on a Baradice,
May theth genen hager dowle,
Ha tha vysshew bras cothys
    Y thone der order an Tas.
    Trew, govy.

A tree in Paradice with a meyd in the topp; and (reching in her armes the Serpent) the Tree wher she was before, and Cayne in Hell, sorowing and crying..

Me a weall an place gloryes,
Han eall yn yet ow sevall,
Splan tha welas ha precyous.
Me a vyn mos pur evall
    En thotha, thy salugy.

Eall Dew an Nef a wartha, 19v
Theis lowena, ha mear joy!
Devethis y thof omma
Gans Adam ow thase thewhy,
    In della mar powgh plesys.

Cherubyn Angell
Seyth, des nes, ha lavar
Tha nagyssyow heb daunger,
    Ha na gymar owne in bys.

Seth
Ow negys y thew hemma:
Tha whelas Oyle a Vercy.
Charges y thof in della
Gans ow thas omma thewhy,
    Ages bothe marsew henna.

1767. temtacion temtacon *MS.*
1769. genen *Nance;* genaf *MS.*
1772 sd. *Serpent) the Tree... crying. this ed; as far as* Serpent *MS (remainder of direction at 1778 (on 19v) in MS).*
1789. Gans ow thas *Stokes;* Ow thas *MS.*

We are chased from Paradise
by the great temptation of the Devil;
we have had a cruel reversal,
and we are fallen into great
misery
by order of the Father.
Alas, woe is me.

A tree in Paradise with a maid in the top; and (the Serpent extended in her branches) the Tree where she was before, and Cain in Hell, sorrowing and crying.

I see the glorious place,
and the angel standing in the gate,
precious and bright to see.
I will go most humbly
even to him, to greet him.

Angel of God of Heaven above,
happiness to you, and great joy!
I have come here
sent to you by Adam my father,
if so you may be pleased.

Cherub, [the] Angel
Come near, Seth, and say
your business without hesitation,
and do not be at all afraid.

Seth
My business is this:
to seek the Oil of Mercy.
I am ordered so
here to you by my father,
if that is your will.

Rag y thew ef cothe gyllys,
Hag in bysma nangew squyth.
Y drobell y thew kemys
Whansack nyngew tha drevyth,
    Mes pub eare ma ow crya
    Warlerth an Oyle a Vercy.

Angell Des nes then yet, Seyth, ha myer.
Te a weall oll Paradice.
Aviece pub tra, ha lavar
Pandra welleth a strangnes
    Yn jarden abarth agy.

Seyth *(Lett Seyth look into Paradice)*
Ages bothe marsew henna,
Me a vyn skon a vycya
    An marodgyan es ena.

Ther he vyseth all thingys, and seeth two trees: and in the one tree sytteth Mary the Virgyn, and in her lappe her sonn Jesus, in the tope of the Tree of Lyf, and, in the other tree, the Serpent which caused Eva to eat the appell.

Angell Lemyn, Seyth, lavar thyma
A bervath pandra welta.
    Na wra kelas un dra.

Seyth Me a weall sure un gwethan,
Ha serpent unhy a vadn.
    Marow seigh hy a valsa.

For he has grown old,
and now he is tired in this world.
His trouble is so great
that he has no desire for anything at all,
except that he is continually
crying out
for the Oil of Mercy.

Angel
Come near to the gate, Seth, and look.
You will see all Paradise.
Take note of everything, and say
what you see that is strange
within the garden.

Seth
(Let Seth look into Paradise)
If that is your will,
I will at once take note
of the marvels that are there.

There he looks at everything, and sees two trees: and in the one tree sits Mary the Virgin, and in her lap her son Jesus, in the top of the Tree of Life, and, in the other tree, the Serpent which caused Eve to eat the apple.

Angel
Now, Seth, tell me
what you see within.
Do not conceal one thing.

Seth
Surely I see a tree,
and a serpent up in it.
It would seem to be dry dead.

Angell

Hona ew an keth wethan
A wrug kyns theth vam ha tas
Debbry an avall a ankan
O defednys gans chardg bras
A anow an Tas gwella.

Han serpent na a welta
Y thew an very pryf na
A wrug an Jowle tha entra
Unny hy rag temtya
Theth vam Eva.

Der henna, Dew a sorras,
Ha tha ve eve a ornas
A lena aga chassya.
Lavar pandra welta moy.

Seyth

Me a weall goodly wythan
Hay thop pur ughall in ban;
Besyn neave ma ow tevy.

Hay gwrethow than door ysall
Yma ow resacke, pur leall,
Besyn Effarn, pytt pur greyf.

Hag ena ow brodar Cayne 20r
Me an gweall ef in mer bayne,
Hag in trobell maythew gwef.

Hag in tope an keth wethan
Me a weall un maytheth wheake
Ow setha, in pur sertan,
Hag in y devra flogh teake,
Der havall thym indella.

1817. pryf na pryfna *Stokes*; pryd na *MS*.
1822. eve *Stokes;* ave *MS*.
1833. trobell trobll *MS*.

Angel

That is the same tree
from which formerly your mother and father
ate the apple of misery
which was forbidden by a strict injunction
from the mouth of the sublime
Father.

And the serpent that you see
is the very same reptile
which the Devil entered
inside in order to tempt
your mother Eve.

Because of that, God was angry,
and he ordered me
to drive them away.
Say what more you see.

Seth

I see a goodly tree
with its top very high up;
it is growing right into Heaven.

And down below its roots
are running, truly,
into Hell, a mighty pit.

And there I see my brother Cain
in great pain,
and in trouble that causes him grief.

And in the top of that same tree
I see a sweet maiden
sitting, most certainly,
and a lovely child in her bosom,
really like myself thus.

Angell

Me a lavar theis dibblance:
Honna (lell y thew henwys)
Ew an Wethan a Vewnans.
Me a heath ran an frutyes,
    Hag a thro parte anetha,
    Avall pur vras.

The Angell goeth to the Tree of Lyf and breaketh an appell, and taketh three coores and geveth yt to Seyth.

Meyr, attomma tayre sprusan
A theth mes an avall ma.
Kemerthy ha goer in ban
In neb tellar tha gova,
    Ha doag y genas theth tas.

Pen vo dewath y thethyow,
Hag in doer tha vos anclythys,
Goer sprusan in y anowe,
Han thew arall kekeffrys
    Bethans gorrys in ye thyw fridg.

Hag y teif an keth spruse na
Un gwethan woȝa hemma,
    Na berth dowt, avyth pur deak.

Ha penvo hy cowle devys,
Hy a vyth pub ear parys
    Tha thone an Oyle a Vercy.

Angel

I will tell you plainly:
that (rightly is it named)
is the Tree of Life.
I shall fetch some of the fruit,
and bring a part of them,
a very large apple.

The Angel goes to the Tree of Life and breaks open an apple, and takes three pips and gives them to Seth.

Look, here are three pips
which came from this apple.
Take them and put them away
somewhere concealed,
and carry them with you to your father.

When it is his ending-day,
and he is to be buried in the earth,
place a pip in his mouth,
and likewise let the other two
be put in his nostrils.

And afterwards a tree
will grow from those very pips
which will be very beautiful, never fear.

And when it is fully grown,
it will be always ready
to bear the Oil of Mercy.

Pan vo pymp myell ha pymp cans
A vlethydnyow clere passhes,
In urna gwaytyans duwhans
Warlerth Oyle Mercy pub pryes,
Ha Salvador in teffry,
An dora mes a baynes.

Lavar theth tas in della,
Ha thotha ythyll trustya.
In delma ythew poyntyes.

Fysten dewhans a lemma.
Ow banneth theis.

Seyth Mear aras thewhy, Eall Due,
Ow tysqwethas thym pub tra.
Thow thas kere oll pardell ew
Me a vyn sure y thysca;
An marogyan dell ew braes.

Me a vyn mos a lema
In hanow Dew a wartha,
Tha dre tha Adam ow thas.

Seyth goes to his father with the coores, and gyveth yt hem.

Lowena thewhy ow thas!
Devethis a Paradice
Y thof lemyn, tha Thew gras.
Ow negyssyow ythew gwryes,
Pardel wrussowgh thym orna.

Adam Welcom os, Seyth, genaf ve. 20v
Pana nowethis es genas?
Marsew an Oyle a Vercy
Dres genas omma theth tas
Pur lowan me a vea.

When five thousand and five hundred
years are quite passed,
at that time let him expect soon
the Oil of Mercy at all times,
and a Saviour indeed,
who will bring him out of pains.

Tell your father so,
and he may trust to it.
It is appointed so.

Hurry away quickly.
My blessing on you.

Seth

Many thanks to you, Angel of God,
for revealing everything to me.
I will surely teach
my dear father everything as it is,
of the wonders, great as they are.

I will go away
in the name of God above,
home to Adam my father.

*Seth goes to his father with
the kernels, and gives them to him.*

Joy to you, my father!
Thanks to God, I am now
come from Paradise.
My business is done,
just as you ordered me.

Adam

You are welcome to me, Seth.
What news do you have?
If the Oil of Mercy has been
brought by you here to your father
I should be very happy.

Seyth Nagew whath, ow thaes, forsothe.
Me a levar thewgh, dell goeth,
An gwreanathe a bub tra.

Pan defa an termyn playne
A pymp myell ha pymp cans vlethan,
An Oyle a Vercye in nena
A vythe kevys.

Yn Paradice y whelys
Defrans marrodgyan, heb dowt;
Specyall un gwethan gloryes
Ow hethas in ban pur stowte
Besyn Nef, sure me agryes,

Hay gwreythow than doer ysall
Besyn Effarn ow hethas,
Hag ena, pur wyer heb fall,
Y thesa in trobell braes
Ow brodar Cayne, in paynes.

Now in toppe an wethan deake
Y thesa un virgyn wheake,
Hay floghe, pur semely maylyes,
Uny defran, wondrys whans.

Adam Gorthis rebo Dew an Taes,
Ow ry thym an nowethys.
Sure nymbef bes vyth mar vraes!
Nangew termyn tremenys
A vlethydnyowe moy es cans.

Seythe Me a wellas gwethan moy
Ha serpent in ban ynny.
Marow seigh hy a falsa.

1915. vlethydnyowe *Stokes*; vlenydnyowe *MS*.

Seth

It isn't, yet, my father, truly.
As is needful, I will tell you
the truth about everything.

When the time shall have plainly come
of five thousand and five hundred years,
at that time the Oil of Mercy
shall be found.

In Paradise I saw
several marvels, really;
especially a glorious tree
reaching proudly up
right to Heaven, I truly believe,

with its roots reaching down below
right into Hell,
and there, really and truly,
in great trouble, was
my brother Cain, in pain.

Now in the top of the lovely tree
was a sweet maiden,
with her child, most beautifully swaddled,
in her bosom, a strangely moving
thing.

Adam

Glory be to God the Father,
for giving me the news.
Surely nothing is more important to me!
Now the time
of more than a hundred years has
passed.

Seth

I saw another tree
with a serpent up in it.
It seemed to be dry dead.

Adam

Honna o drog preyf, heb nam,
A dullas Eva tha vabm.
Der henna I kylsyn jam
    Joyes Paradice rag nefra.

Seyth

Attomma tayr sprusan, dryes
Mes a Baradice thewhy.
A avall yfons terrys
A theth an wethan, defry,
    Ew henwys Gwethan a Vewnans.

An Eall a ornas thevy,
Panvo dewath theth dythyow
Hath voes gyllys a lema,
Gorra sprusan yth ganow,
    Han thew arall pur thybblance
    In tha thew freyge.

Mes an spruse y fyth tevys 21r
Gwethan a vyth pure precyous
    Wosa henna, marthys teake
    In pur theffry.

Ha penvo hy cowle devys,
Hy a vyth pub eare parys
    Tha thone an Oyle a Vercye.

Adam

Mere worthyans than Drenges Tase
Ow crowntya thymmo sylwans,
    Woȝa hemma ken thew pell.

Seyth ow mabe, golsow themma,
Ha theth chardgya me ara
    In dan ow bannethe, pur leall:

Adam

That was an evil snake, indeed,
that tricked your mother Eve.
Through that we have now lost
the joys of Paradise for ever.

Seth

Here are three pips, brought
to you out of Paradise.
They were picked from an apple
that came, indeed, from the tree
that is named the Tree of Life.

The Angel ordered me,
when your ending-day has come
and you have departed,
to put a pip in your mouth,
and the other two separately
into your nostrils.

From the pips will be grown
a tree that will be very precious
hereafter, wonderfully lovely
in very truth.

And when it is fully grown,
it will be always ready
to bear the Oil of Mercy.

Adam

Great honour to the Father in Trinity
for granting me salvation,
even though it be long hereafter.

Hear me, my son Seth,
and I charge you
faithfully, under my blessing:

Gwayte an Tas an Nef gorthya,
Ha pub ere orta cola
Yn pub otham a vesta.
Ef a wra sure tha succra,
Hag a vydn tha vayntaynya
In bysma pell tha vewa.
    Ow mabe, merke an gyrryow ma.

Seyth
A das kere, mere rase thewhy
Agys dyscans da pub preyse.
Me agoth in pur thefrye
Gorthya Dew an leall Drengys,
    Han Mabe gwelha,

Han Spyryssans, aga thry.
Dell yns onyn, me a gryes
Try fersons yns, pur worthy,
Ow kys raynya in joyes
    In gwlase Nef es a wartha.

Ha rag henna y coth thyma
Gans colan pure aga gwerthya.

Lett Death apeare to Adam.

Adam
Coth ha gwan ythof gyllys;
Nym beas bewa na fella.
Ankaw ythew devethys.
Ny vyn omma ow gasa
    Tha vewa omma udn spyes.

Me an gweall prest gans gew,
Parys thom gwana pub tew.
    Nygeas scappya deva;
    An preys mallew genaf.

Take care to worship the Father of Heaven,
and always trust to him
in every need you may have.
He will surely aid you,
and will maintain you
to live long in this world.
Mark these words, my son.

Seth

O dear father, many thanks to you
for your good teaching at all
times.
Most truly I ought
to worship God of the true Trinity,
and the best Son,

and the Holy Spirit, they three.
As they are one, I believe
they are three persons, most worthy,
reigning together in joy
in the land of Heaven above.

And therefore I ought
to worship them with a pure heart.

Let Death appear to Adam.

Adam

I have grown old and weak;
I have no longer to live.
Death has come.
He will not leave me here
to live here for one moment.

I see him with a dart,
always ready to pierce me on all sides.
There is no escaping for me;
I am glad of the time.

Me a servyas pell an beyse,
Aban vema kyns formys.
Naw cans bloth of, me a gryes,
Ha deakwarnegans, recknys,
    May thew pryes mos a lema.

Flehys ambef denethys 21v
A Eva ow freas mear:
Dewthack warnygans genys
A vibbyan (hemma ew gwyre),
    Heb ow mabe Cayne, hag Abell.

Yn weth dewthak warnugans
A virhas in pur thibblans
    Ny anbe, heb tull na gyll,
    A thalathfas an bysma.

Han bys ythew incresshys
Drethaf ve hag ow flehys
Heb nunnber tha vos comptys:
    Tha Thew y whom gras ractha.

Death Adam, gwra thymmo parys:
Te am gweall ve devethys
    Theth vewnans gans ow spera

The gameras a lemma.
Nynges gortas na fella;
Rag henna gwra theth wana,
    Deran golan may thella.

    Death smyteth hem with his spear,
    and he falleth upon a bead.

1999 sd. *at 1995 in MS: not in Stokes.*

5. *The Death of Adam*, panel 14 of *The Creation Window*.

I have long served the world,
since I was first formed.
I am nine hundred years old, I believe,
and thirty, all told,
and it is time to go.

I have many children born
of Eve my wife:
produced thirty-two
sons (this is true),
besides my son Cain, and Abel.

Also thirty-two
daughters exactly
have we had, in all honesty,
since the beginning of the world.

And the world has increased
through me and my children
without number to be counted:
I give thanks to God therefore.

Death Adam, make ready for me:
you see that I have come
to take away

your life with my spear.
There is no waiting any longer;
therefore I shall pierce you,
to penetrate the heart.

Death strikes him with his spear,
and he falls on a bed.

Adam

Ankow, y whon theis mer grace
Ow bewnans tha gameras
    Mes an bysma,

Rag pursqwyth ove anotha.
Tha Thew y whon gras ragtha.

Gwyn ow bys bos thym fethys
Lavyr ha dewhan an beyse.
    Pel me ren servyas omma.

Ha rag henna gwraf comena
Then leall Drengys ow ena.

First Devyll

Cowetha, bethowgh parys,
An thevillow pub onyn!
Ena Adam tremenys:
Dune thy hethas than gegen,
    Then pytt downe barth a wollas.

Lucyfer

Na, na, ny wreth in della!
Yma ken ornes ractha.
Yn Lymbo, barth a wartha
Ena ef a wra trega,
    Del ew ornes gans an Tace.

Ty a wore in Effarnowe
Yma mansyons, heb gow,
Neb yma an thewollow
A theth mes an Nef golow
    Genaf ve ow toen rowle vras:

2007. servyas *conj. Stokes;* sewyas *MS.*
2011. thevillow thevllow *MS.*

6. *Hell kitchen, from The Holkham Bible Picture Book*, BL MS 47682, f42^{v}.

Adam

Death, I thank you greatly
for taking my life
from this world,

for very weary I am of it.
I give thanks to God therefore.

I am lucky that for me
the toil and trouble of the world are overcome.
I have long served it here.

And therefore I do commend
to the true Trinity my soul.

[Some devils emerge from Hell.]

First Devil

Get you ready, boys,
every one of the devils!
The soul of dead Adam:
let's go and fetch it to the kitchen,
to the deep pit down below.

Lucifer

No, no, you mustn't do that!
There are different arrangements for him.
He will stay there
in Limbo, up above,
as was ordained by the Father.

You know that in Hell's domains,
where the devils are
who came out of bright Heaven
holding high authority with me,
there are mansions, in truth:

An chorll Adam y drygva 22r
A vyth abarth a wartha
In onyn an clowster na,
Neb na vyth tam lowena,
Mes in tewolgow bras ena
    Ow kelly presens an Tase,

Han moygha payne a vetha
Y vabe Cayne; in paynes brase
Ef a dryg bys venytha.
Yma ef barth a wollas,
    In pytt downe ow leskye.

Third devyll
Praga na vyth an chorle Adam
In kethe della tremowntys?
Me a wra then horsen cam
Boos calassa presonys
    Mar callaf, kyns es hethy,
    Drefan terry gorhemyn.

Lucyfer
Me a lavar theis an case.
Kyn wrug Adam pegh mar vras,
    Ef an geva yddrage tyn,

Ha Dew thothef a avas
Y thyspleasur hay sor bras,
    Hag in della ny wrug Cayne.

Ef a lathas ye vrodar
Ny gemeras yddrag vyth,
Mes y regoyssyas pur vear,
Hag a sor an Tas trevythe
    Yn serten ef ny synges.

the home of that wretch Adam
will be up above
in one of those cloisters,
where there will not be a scrap of joy,
but being deprived of the Father's
presence
there in great darkness,

and the greatest pain shall
his son Cain have; in great pain
he will stay forever.
There he is below
burning in a deep pit.

Third devil

Why won't the wretch Adam be
tormented in the same way?
I'll have the evil bastard
be most securely imprisoned
right away, if I can,
since he broke the commandment.

Lucifer

I'll tell you how it is.
Though Adam committed a very grave sin,
he repented keenly,

and God forgave him
his indignation and his great wrath,
and Cain did not do that.

He killed his brother
and had no repentance at all,
but greatly rejoiced,
and certainly he cared nothing
at all for the wrath of God.

Rag henna bys venary
Eve a dryg ena deffry
In paynes bras, a vel ky.
    Joy Nef ew thotha kellys.

Yea, Cayne hay gowetha
In keth order a vewa.
An place yw ornes ractha
    In Efarn barth a wollas.

Hag Adam (vengens thotha!) -
Lymbo ew ornys ractha,
Ea, ragtha ef hay gowetha.
    Ny dastyans an payne bras.

They go to Hell with great noyes.

First Devyll
Ytholl agen vyadge ny,
Ren jowle bras, ny dalvyth oye!
    Tregans an chorle neb yma.

Dune ny war barth, a gowetha,
Tha Effarnow a lema,
    Then paynes a thewre nefra.

An Angell conveyeth Adam's soole to Lymbo.

[*Angell*]
A ena Adam dremas,
Des genaf ʒa Effarnow.
Ena ornys thies ew place
Gans an Tas, theso, heb gowe,
    Tha remaynya rag season.

2063. hay ha[y] *Stokes*; ha *MS.*
2064 sd. *so placed in Nance; at 2056 in MS.*
2071 sd. *so placed in Nance; at 2061-4 in MS.*
2071 sp. *Stokes; not in MS.*

Eternally therefore
he will surely stay there
like a dog, in great pain.
The joy of Heaven is lost to him.

Yes, Cain and his like
will live under that dispensation.
The place is ordained for him
down below in Hell.

And (curse him!) Adam -
Limbo is ordained for him,
yes, for him and his like.
They will not taste the great pain.

They go to Hell with great noise.

First Devil Then all our venture
isn't worth an egg, by the great devil!
Let the wretch stay where he is.

Let's go together, boys,
away to Hell's domains,
to the pains that last forever.

An Angel carries Adam's soul to Limbo.

[Angel] O soul of good Adam,
come with me to Hell's domains.
A place is ordained for you there
by the Father, truly, for you
to remain for a time.

Pan deffa an Oyle a Vercy, 22v
Te avith kerrys then joye
Than Nef ughall a ughan.

Lett Adam be buried in a fayre tombe with som churche songys at hys buryall.

Seythe

Ow thas pan ewa marowe
Me a vyn y anclythyas.
Dun a lebma heb falladow;
Gorryn an corf in gweras
Gans solempnyty ha cane.

Mes an dore eve ave gwryes,
Hag arta then keth gwyrras
Ef avyth treylyes serten.

Ha del ve thym kyns ornys,
An dayer sprusan yw gorrys
In y anow hay fregowe.

The three kernels put in his mowthe and nostrells.

Del o ef an kensa dean
A ve gans an Tas fornyes,
Yn beth yta ef lebmyn.
Then Tas Dew rebo grassies
Oma rag y oberowe.

Enoch

Enoch ythew owe hanowe,
Leall servant then Drengis Tas.
Mabe Jared ythov, heb gowe,
Sevys a lydnyathe pur vras
Heb dowt ythof.

2078 sd. *so placed in Stokes; at 2071-5 (on 22r) in MS.*
2089 sd. *at 2086-9 in MS.*

When the Oil of Mercy shall come,
you will be brought to the joy
in Heaven high above us.

Let Adam be buried in a fine tomb, with some church songs at his burial.

Seth

Since my father is dead
I shall bury him.
Let us come away without fail;
let us set the body in the ground
with ceremonial song.

From the earth he was made,
and to that same ground again
he shall be turned for certain.

And as I was ordered before
the three pips are put
in his mouth and his nostrils.

The three kernels put in his mouth and nostrils.

As he was the first man
who was formed by God,
behold him now in a grave.
Thanks be to God the Father
for his work here.

[Another part of the place.]

Enoch

Enoch is my name,
loyal servant to the Father in Trinity.
I am the son of Jared, in truth,
no doubt I am
sprung from a mighty lineage.

Ha, pur leall, an sythvas degre
Desendys a Adam ove.
In oydg me ew in ourma
Try cans try ugans in prove,
    Ha whath pymp moy, pan es thym coof,
    In geth hythew.

Me a beys tha wrear Neffe
May fon pub eare plegadow
Tha vonas y servant ef
In bysma heb falladowe
    Ha drevone bewe.

Father in Heaven

Enoch *(Enoch kneleth when the Father speketh)* me a levar thyes
Ow bothe tha vos in delma:
May fosta qwyck transformys.
Tha Baradice a lemma
Me a vyn may foes uskys
Hethis in corf hag ena.
    Byth parys in termyn ma.

Hag ena y wres gortas
Ogas tha worvan an beyse.
An mystery ythew pur vras;
Genaf nyvyth dysclosyes
    Tha thean vytholl in bysma.

Enoche is caried to Paradice.

2111 sd. *at 2104 in MS.*
2116. Hethis *(Nance)*; [b]ethis *Stokes; blot on first two letters in MS.*

And, in all faith, of the seventh degree
descended from Adam am I.
At this moment I am of age
three hundred and sixty indeed,
and five more besides, now I think of it,
on this very day.

I pray to the maker of Heaven
that I may always have the pleasure
to be his servant
unfailingly in this world
as long as I live.

Father in Heaven

Enoch *(Enoch kneels when the Father speaks)* I say to you
that my will is thus:
that you be translated alive.
I wish that you be immediately
taken in body and soul
from here to Paradise.
Be ready at this time.

And there you will wait
till nearly the end of the world.
The mystery is very great;
it will not be disclosed by me
unto anyone at all in the world.

Enoch is carried to Paradise.

Enoch Gorthyes rebo Dew an Tas! 23r
Tha vlonogath rebo gwryes.
Hemma ythew marrudgyan bras:
Y thesaf ow pose gorthys
    Ny won pylea.

Me a wore hag a leall gryes
Gwreans Dew y vos hemma.
Devethys tha Baradice
Me a wore gwyre y thoma.
    Place delycyous ew hemma;
    Peldar ynno me a vewe.

Der temptacion an teball
Ow hendas Adam, pur weare
Eave regollas, der avall,
An place gloryous pur sure,
    Maythew gweve oll thy asshew.

Rag henna, pobell an beise,
Na wreugh terry an deffan
A vyth gans Dew thugh ornys,
Dowte tha gawas drog gorfan
    Ha myschef bras war bub tew.

Mara qwrewgh orthaf cola
Why asbythe woȝa hemma
    Joies Nef in udn rew.

Seyth Kebmys pehas es in byes
Gwrres gans tues heb amendya,
Mathew Dew an Tas serrys
Bythqwath gwyell mabe dean omma.

2142. tha *Stokes' reading;* that *MS.*

Enoch

Glory be to God the Father!
Your will be done.
This is a great miracle:
I am being placed
I know not where.

I know and faithfully believe
this to be God's doing.
I know well that I have
come to Paradise.
This is a delightful place;
I shall live in it for a long time.

Through the temptation of the evil one
my forefather Adam, truly
he lost, by an apple,
the glorious place for certain,
and there is grief for all his offspring.

Therefore, people on earth,
do not break the commandment
that is ordained to you by God,
lest you come to a bad end
and great trouble all round.

If you heed me
you will have hereafter
the joys of Heaven eternally.

Seth

So many sins in the world have been
done by men without retribution,
that God the Father is angry
for ever making man here.

Distructyon yma ornys
Pur serten war oll an beise,
May fyth consumys pub tra.

Henna ythew convethys
Der an discans es thymma reis
Gans an Tas es a ughan.

An planattys es a wartha,
Han steare inweth magata,
Ow poyntya mowns pur efan.

Let hem poynt to the sun, the moone, and the firmament.

An howle han loor kekeffrys,
Oll warbarth ew confethys,
Than purpose na mowns ow toos.

Han distructyon a vyth bras,
May fyth an byes destryes
Der levyaw a thower pur vras,
Po der dane yfyth leskys.
Cresough thyma marsowhy fure.

Rag henna gwrens tues dowtya
An tase Dew tha offendya
Der neb maner for in beyse.

Rag voydya an perill na, 23v
Scryffes yma thym pub tra
A thallathfas an bysma,
May fova leall recordys
A vyns tra es ynna gwryes.

Destruction is ordained
for certain the whole world over,
and everything will be consumed.

That is understood
through the learning that has been given to me
by the Father above us.

The planets above,
and the stars as well too,
are setting it out very plainly.

Let him point to the sun, the moon and the firmament.

The sun and the moon too,
which are all together comprehended,
are gathering for that purpose.

And the destruction will be vast,
and the world will be destroyed
by tremendous floods of water,
or it will be burnt by fire.
Believe me if you are wise.

Therefore let men fear
to offend God the Father
in any sort of way in the world.

In order to neutralise that danger,
I have had everything written down
from the beginning of this world,
so that it be truly recorded
about everything that has been done in it.

Four bookes to be shewed.

An leverow y towns y omma -
Why as gweall, wondrys largya;
Ha pub tra oll in bysma
Skryffes yma in ryma,
Dowt navons y ankevys.

Deaw pillar manaff poyntya
Rag an purpas na whare.
Bryck a vyth onyn anotha,
Ha marbell avith y gylla.
Rag sawment y avyth gwryes
Than leverowe.

Two pyllars made, the on of brick and thother of marbell.

An bricke rag navons leskys
Der dane vyth, henna ew gwryes,
Han marbell tam consumys
Der thower ny vyth, hema ew gwyer,
Drefan y vos mean garow,
Wondrys callys.

Jared

An pillars y towns parys:
Gorowgh ynna an leverow.
Nynges art vyth ankevys,
Na tra arall, sure heb ow,
Mes unna mowns skryves.

2191-2. *so placed in Stokes; after 2188 in MS.*

Four books to be showed.

Observe the books here -
amazingly big, you see them;
and everything in all this world
is written down in these,
lest it should be forgotten.

I shall set up two pillars
immediately for this purpose.
One of them will be of brick,
and the other will be of marble.
They shall be made as a safeguard
for the books.

Two pillars made, the one of brick,
and the other of marble.

The brick, this is made so that they cannot be
burnt by fire at all,
and the marble will not be worn away a bit
by water, this is the truth,
because of its being a rough stone,
wonderfully hard.

Jared

Behold the pillars ready:
place the books in them.
There is no art at all forgotten,
nor anything besides, in certain truth,
that is not written in them.

A bub sort oll a leverow
Egwall unna ew gorrys,
Pekare ythew an sortow
Gorrys unna der devyes,
    In diffrans ha kehavall.

Lemyn me as goer in badn,
Hag in nyell sure bys vickan
    An record a vythe heb fall
    Pur wyer kevys.
    Putt the pillers upright.

Seyth

Rag henna pobell dowtyans,
Ha then Tas gwren oll pegy
Na skydnya an keth vengeans
In neb termyn warnan ny
    Nagen flehys.

Father in Heaven

Drog ew genaf gwythill dean,
Preshyous havall thom honyn.
Rag cola orthe udn venyn
    Glane ef regollas an place

Am leff dyghow a wrussen.
Pan wrega dryes ow defen
Mes a Baradice pur glane
    Whare an eall as gorras.

An sperys ny drige neffra 24r
In corf mabe dean vyth in byes.
Ha reason ew ha praga,
Rag y voos kyg medall gwryes,
    Ha pur vrotall gans henna.

2213. havall *(Nance)*; havan *MS*.
2216. a wrussen *Nance*; pan wrussen *MS*.

Material from every variety of all books
is put equally in each,
just as the varieties of
information
are put into them according to a plan,
different and the same.

Now I shall set them upright,
and surely forever in one of the two
the record will unfailingly
be truly found.

Put the pillars upright.

Seth

Therefore let people fear,
and let us all pray to the Father
that the same vengeance may not descend
at any time upon us
nor our children.

Father in Heaven

I am sorry that I made man,
precious like to myself.
For listening to a woman
he has quite lost the place

which I had made with my right hand.
When he acted against my prohibition
the angel at once put them
right out of Paradise.

The spirit will not live forever
in the body of any man in the world.
And it is right and reason,
because of his being made of soft flesh,
and very frail with it.

Nynges dean orthe ow servya
Len ha gwyrryan sure pub pryes
Saw Noye in oll an bysma
Hay wreag hay flehys keffrys.
  Ow bothe ythew in della:

Gweyll deall war oll an byes
May fythe pub tra consumys;
  Mes serten mannaf sawya.

Noy Noy, mabe Lamec, gylwys ove:
Arluthe brase, oll perthew cove,
  Ythof, omma in bysma.

Substance lowere a byth ha da
Yma thyma tha vewa,
May thof sengys rag neffra
Tha worthya ow Arluth da,
  An Drengys es a wartha.

Father in Heaven Noye, des thymma ve lebmyn,
Ha golsow thym a gowsaf.

Noy commeth before Heven and kneleth.

Noy Parys ove, Arluthe brentyn;
Tha vlonogathe lavartha.

2243 sd. *at 2240 in MS.*

There is no man serving me
loyally and truly indeed at all times
except Noah in all this world,
and his wife and his children too.
My will is thus:

to take vengeance over all the world
so that everything will be consumed.
But I mean to save certain people.

[Enter Noah.]

Noah

I am called Noah, son of Lamech:
I am a great lord, everyone remember,
here in this world.

I have sufficient means of goods and chattels
to live on,
so that I am forever bound
to honour my good Lord,
of the Trinity above.

Father in Heaven

Come to me now, Noah,
and hear what I shall say.

Noah comes in front of Heaven and kneels.

Noah

I am ready, noble Lord:
speak your will.

Father in Heaven

Noy, mar lenwys ew an byes
Lemyn a sherewynsy
May thew dewathe devethys
Unna a gyke pub hunythe.
Gans peagh pur wyre ew flayrys.
Ny allaf sparya namoye
Heb gwethill mernans a vear spyes
War pobell oll menas tye
Ha tha wreag hatha flehys,
Han pythe a long theȝo gye.

Tooles and tymber redy, with planckys to make the Arcke: a beam, a mallet, a calkyn yre, ropes, mastes, pyche, and tarr.

Rag henna fysten, ke gwra
Gorthell a planckes playnyes,
Hag unna leas trigva
Rowmys y a vythe henwys.
A veas hag agy inta
Gans peyke bethance stanche gwryes.
Ha try cans kevellyn da
An lysster a vythe in heys.

Ha hantercans kevellen
Inweth te a wra yn leas,
Han uheldar me a vyn
Deagwarnygans may fo gwryes.
War tew a thella, daras -
Ea - ty a wra: port ef a vyth henwys.
Jystes dretha ty a place,
A leas rag navo degys.

2254 sd. *at 2255-74 in MS.*
mastes this ed; masses *MS.*
mass[t]es Stokes.
2269. place *Stokes;* playne *MS.*

Father in Heaven

Noah, the world is so full
of wickedness now
than an end has come
for every kind of flesh in it.
It is truly stinking with sin.
I can refrain no longer
from visiting death shortly
on all people except you
and your wife and your children,
and the things that belong to you.

Tools and timber ready, with planks to make the Ark: a beam, a mallet, a caulking iron, ropes, masts, pitch, and tar.

Therefore hurry, go and make
an ark from planed planks,
with many living areas in it -
they shall be called rooms.
Let it be made watertight with pitch
thoroughly without and within.
And a good three hundred cubits
the ship will be in length.

And also you shall make it
fifty cubits wide,
and I want the height
to be made thirty.
Aft, a door -
aye - you will make: it shall be called a port.
You will place joists through it,
that it may not come wide open.

A bub ehan a gynda
Gorrow ha benaw in wethe:
Aga gorra ty a wra
In tha lester a bervathe.

Pub maner boos in bysma
Es ȝa thybbry gwayte may treythe;
Rag dean ha beast magata,
In tha lester gweyt may fethe.

Noye

Arluthe kref, tha arhadowe 24v
Me ara, so mot y go.
Ow lythyow, heb falladowe,
Me a vyn dallathe strechya.

Gans ow boell nowyth lemmys
Me a squat pub pice tymber,
Hag a pleyne oll an planckes,
Haga sett pub plyenkyn sure.

Sem

Me a galke thew wondres fyne
Nagella dower vyth ynno.
Kyn fova gwryes a owerbyn,
Yfyth stanche, me a ragtha.

Cham

Yma peyke thym provyes,
Ha lavonowe pub ehan.
Deffrans sortowe a wernow
Yma parys pur effan.

2276. may m[a]y *Stokes;* my *MS.*
2281. Ow lythyow *Nance;* Turlythyow *MS.*
2293. Deffrans *Stokes;* dreffrans *MS.*

A male and a female also
from every kind of species:
you will put them
within your ship.

See that you bring every kind of
food in the world
that is to eat;
see that it be in your ship
for man and beast as well.

Noah

On my life, I shall do
your bidding, mighty Lord.
I will begin to stretch
my limbs, without fail.

With my newly-sharpened axe
I will chop every piece of timber,
and plane all the planks,
and fix every plank securely.

[Enter Shem, Ham, and Japheth.]

Shem

I will caulk extremely carefully for you
so that no water at all may get into it.
Even if it should rain overhead
it will be watertight, I'll
vouch for that.

Ham

Here is pitch procured for me,
and ropes of every kind.
Different sorts of masts -
they are ready in evidence.

Tuball Cayn

Marthe ew genaf a un dra:
Y vosta mar ucky, Noye.
Praga ew genas she omma
Buyldya lester mar worthy
In creys powe, tha worthe an moare?

Lett Tuball fall a laughing.

Me a syns tha skeans whath,
Tha voes in cost an parna!
Oll tha lyvyer nyn dale cathe,
Me an to war owe ena!
Gucky y thoes.

Noy

Ow hothman, na gybmar marthe;
Ty an oole, ha lyas myell.
Kynthota skydnys in wharthe,
In dewathe, heb tull na gyle,
Why a weall deall uskys.

Gwarnys of gans Dew an Tase
Tha wythell an lesster ma,
Rag ow sawya haw flehys
Tha worthe an kethe deall na.
Why a weall agy tha space
Der lyvyow a thower an brassa
Oll an beise a vyth bethys.

Jabell

Gwell vea a vosta kregys,
Ty hag oll an grydgyans na!
A chorll coth, te pedn pylles,
Fatla vynta ge henna;
Y fythe an beys consumys?
Oll an dorrowe in beysma,
Kynfons warbarthe contylles
Ny wra dewath an parna!

2299 sd. *laughing* laughng *MS.*
2318. grydgyans *Stokes;* grydgyan *MS.*
2320. Fatla *Stokes;* flatla *MS.*

[Enter Tubalcain and Jabel.]

Tubalcain

There is one thing that astounds me:
that you are so stupid, Noah.
Why has it got into you here
to build such a splendid ship
in the middle of the country, away from the sea?

Let Tubal start laughing.

I give a fart for your wisdom,
to go to such a cost!
All your work isn't worth a cat,
I swear it on my soul!
You're mad!

Noah

Do *not* be astounded, my friend;
you will weep for it, and many thousands.
Although you have fallen to laughing,
in the end, and I'm telling the truth,
you will see a swift vengeance.

I have been warned by God the Father
to make this ship,
in order to save myself and my children
from that same vengeance.
In a while you will see
that all the world will be drowned
by the most tremendous floods of water.

Jabel

It would be better for you to be hanged,
you and all of that belief!
Oh old wretch, you bald-pate,
where do you get that idea,
that the world will be consumed?
All the waters in this world,
even if they were gathered together
will not cause an end like that!

Sow y thota gy gockye
Oll an beyse a yll gothvas.
Vengans wartha ben krehy!
Nynges omma dean in wlase
   A greys thys malbe vanna.

Praga, pandrew an matter? 25r
A vyn Dew buthy an beise?
Mara custa, thym lavar
An occasyon, me athe pyes,
   Der vaner da.

Noy

An occasion ew hemma:
Kemmys pehas es in beyse,
Ha nynges tam amendya,
Maythew an Tas Dew serrys
   Gans oll pobell an bysma.

Hag eddrag thothef yma
Bythqwath mabe dean tha vos gwryes.
Rag henna gwrewgh amendya;
Ages foly byth nehys.
Yn urna, der vanar da,
Mara pethowgh repentys,
   An kethe plage a wra voydya.

Tuball

Pew athe wrug ge progowther
Tha thesky omma theny?
Y praytha, thymma lavar,
A wrug cowsall thagye
   Only, heb dean arall vyth omma?

2329. thys *(Nance)*; thybm *MS*.

But all the world can see
that you are a fool.
Curses on your lousy head!
There isn't a man here in the land
who'll believe you a damn bit.

Why, what's the matter?
Does God want to drown the world?
Tell me, if you can,
the cause, I entreat you,
in a nice manner.

Noah This is the cause:
so much sin is in the world,
and there is not a speck of atonement,
that God the Father is angry
with all people in the world.

And he repents
that man was ever made.
Therefore make atonement;
be renounced of your folly.
If you will be repentent,
in a nice manner, then
this same punishment will pass away.

Tubal Who made you a preacher
to teach us here?
Tell me, I entreat you,
did he speak to you
only, without any other man here?

Me a wore yma in pow
Leas dean agowse an Tase;
Tues perfyt, me an advow,
Ythyns I, ha polatys brase,
A wayt boos in favour Dew.

Sera, tha radn an ry na
Ef a vynsa disclosya
An distructyon brase han lywe.

Rag henna theth cregye
Me ny vannaf moye es kye.
Na mendya ny venyn ny,
A woos theth gyrryaw wastys.

Noy Da ew theso gy boes fure,
Hag oll pobell an bysma.
Ny vyth Dew nefra pur wyre
Kevys goacke, trest thymo.
Ragtha bethowh a vysshes.

Mar nywrewh, vengence pur vras
A skydn warnowgh kyns na pell,
Rag Dew a vyn, agen Tase,
Danven lywe a thower pur leall,
Serten tha vethy an byese.

Rag omsawya ow honyn,
Keffrys ow gwreak haw flehys,
An lester a vythe genyn
Der weras Dew uskes gwryes,
Rag voydya an danger ma.

Jabell Tety valy, bram an gathe!
My ny gresaf theȝo whathe,
Y fydn Dew gwill in della.

I know there are many men in the country
to whom the Father speaks;
perfect men, I admit it,
they are, and grand fellows,
who expect to be in God's favour.

He would have disclosed,
Sir, to some of them
the great destruction and the flood.

Therefore I shall not believe you
more than a dog.
Nor do we have any intention of atoning,
in spite of your wasted words.

Noah It's for your good to be wise,
and all people of this world.
Certainly God will never
be found a liar, believe me.
Therefore be warned.

If you do not, very great vengeance
will descend on you before not very long,
for God, our Father, will
send a flood of water, truly,
to drown the world for certain.

In order to save myself,
also my wife and my children,
the ship will be made by us
quickly through the help of God,
so as to overcome this danger.

Jabel *Tety valy,* the cat's fart!
I still don't believe you,
that God will do that.

Me a woer ny wrug an beys 25v
Han bobell myns es unna
Tha voos mar qwicke destryes.
Unpossyble ythewa
    An dower na tha vose kevys.

Noy

Unpossyble nyngew tra
Tha Wrear oll an bysma,
A wos destrowy an beyse
    Agy tha ower.

Rag der gear oll a ve gwryes,
Nef ha noer, myns es omma,
Ha der gear arta, thym creys,
Ef a yll, mar a mynna,
    Y thystrowy der an dower.

Tuball

Ny amownt thymma resna
Genas, Noy, me a hevall.
Me a vyn mos a lemma,
Rag y thota droge eball
    Na vyn nefra bonas vase.

Pyrra foole neve gwelys:
Me a levar theis praga.
An lester ew dallethys,
Why a woer, nangew polta,
    A vlethydnyow pur leas
    Moy es ugans.

Rag mar vras yw dallethis
Neffra ny vithe dowethis,
    Me anto warow honssyans.
    Lett them both depart.

I know he didn't make the world
and all people that are in it
to be destroyed so quickly.
It's impossible
for that water to be found.

Noah

Nothing is impossible
for the Creator of all this world,
even to destroy the world
within an hour.

For all was made through a word,
Heaven and earth, everything that is here,
and, believe me, through a word again
he can, if he should wish,
destroy it with the water.

Tubal

It does me no good to reason
with you, Noah, it seems to me.
I shall go away,
for you're an unbridled buck
that will never behave.

A verier fool has never been seen:
I'll tell you why.
The ship was begun
a long while ago now, you know,
a good many years -
more than twenty.

For it has started so big
it will never be finished,
I swear it on my conscience.

Let them both depart.

The Arck redy, and all maner of beastys and fowles to be putt in the Arck.

Noy

Now an lester ythew gwryes,
Teake ha da thom plegadow.
A bub ehan a vestas
Drewhy quick ȝym orthe copplow;
Chattell, ethyn kekeffrys,
Dew ha dew, benaw ha gorrawe.

Sem

Nynges beast na preif in beyse,
Benaw ha gorawe omma,
Genaf thewhy yma dreys.
In lester y towns ena.

Let rayne appeare.

Cham

A dase, lemyn gwrewh parys,
An lyw nangew devethys!
Yma lowar dean in beyse
Kyns lemyn sure a gowȝes
Ages bos why gucky.

Pan wressowh gwyle an lester
Oma prest in creys an tyer,
Moer vyth nyngeȝa, deffry,
The doen in ker.

Japheth

Geas a wressans an notha:
Dowte sor Dew nyngessa
Thothans nena, me a wore gwyer.

The Ark ready, with all kinds of animals and birds to be put in the Ark.

Noah
Now the ship is made,
good and solid to my satisfaction.
Bring me quickly in pairs
some of every kind of beast;
cattle, also birds,
two by two, male and female.

Shem
Every beast and worm in the world,
male and female here,
are brought to you by me.
See them there on board.

Let rain appear.

Ham
O father, make ready now,
the flood has now come!
There is many a man in the world
who surely said before now
that you were mad.

When you made the ship
right here in the middle of the land
there was certainly no sea
to carry it away.

Japhet
They made a joke out of it:
they did not have any fear of the anger of God
then, I know well.

Noye

An lywe nangew devethis, 26r
May thew da thyne fystena.
Pub beast oll yma gyllys
In lester thaga hydnda,
Dell yw ornys thymo ve.

Kewgh a bervath, ow flehys,
Hages gwregath magata.
Ogas an noer ew cuthys
Der an glawe es a wartha.
Te, benyn, a bervathe des;
Ow der bethy a vynta?

Noyes Wiff

Res ew sawya an pyth es:
Nyn dale thym towlall the veas...
Da ew thyn aga sawya.

I costyans showre a vona,
An keth tacklowe es omma,
Noy wheake, te a wore hedna.

A raven and a culver ready.

Noy

Nangew mear a for, pur wyer,
Aban gylsen sight an tyre.
Rag henna thym, te brane vrase,

Nyedge in ker lemyn *(lett the raven fle, and the colver after)* ha myer
Terathe mar kyll bos kevys.
Hag an golan in pur sure
Me as danven pur uskys,
Sight an noer mar kill gwelas.

2448 sd. *so placed in Stokes; at 2445 in MS.*
2452 sd. *at 2448 in MS.*

7. *The Ark Afloat*, from Bristol University Drama Department's production of the *Ordinalia* in Piran Round, 1969.

Noah

The flood has now come,
and we had better hurry.
Every beast has gone
into the ship according to its kind,
as was commanded me.

Go inside, my children,
and your wives as well.
The earth is nearly covered
by the rain that is overhead.
[*Calling to his wife*] You come in, woman;
do you want to be quite drowned?

Noah's Wife

I must save what there is:
I ought not to throw away...
it is good for us to save them.

They cost a shower of money,
these particular items here,
Noah dear, you know that.
[*She boards the Ark.*]

A raven and a dove ready.

Noah

Now it is a great way, truly,
since we lost sight of the land.
Therefore, you raven,

fly away now *(let the raven fly away, and the dove afterwards)* and see
if land can be found.
And most surely I will send the dove
very quickly,
in case she can see a glimpse of the earth.

Father in Heaven

Marowe ew pub tra eʒa
Sperys a vewnans unna.
Me a worhemyn whare
Than glawe namoy na wrella.

The culver commeth with a branche of olyf in her mowthe.

Noy

Then Tase Dew rebo grassyes!
An golan ew devethys,
Ha gensy branche olyf glase.

Arall bethans delyverys.
Does ny vydnas an vrane vras;
Neb caryn hy a gafas.

Nangew ogas ha blethan
Aban dallathfas an lywe.
Marsew bothe Dew y honyn,
Neb ew gwrear noer ha Neef,
Tha slackya an kyth lywe brase,

Y vothe rebo collenwys
Omma genan ny pub pryes,
Kekefrys ha mabe ha tase.

Father in Heaven

Noy, me a worhemyn theis,
Ke in meas an lester skon,
Thethe wreag hathe flehis keffrys,
Ethyn, bestas, ha pub lodn.

Noy

Meare worthyans thyes, Arluth Nef. 26v
Te a weras gwadn ha creaf
In otham, sure, panvo reys.

Father in Heaven

Dead is everything
in which was the spirit of life.
At once I will command
the rain that it rain no more.

The dove comes with a branch of olive in her mouth.

Noah

Thanks be to God the Father!
The dove has come,
and a green olive-branch with her.

Let another be set free.
The raven did not want to come;
it has found some carrion.

Now it is nearly a year
since the beginning of the flood.
If it is the will of God himself,
who is maker of earth and Heaven,
to abate this great flood,

May his will be done
here by us always,
both son and father.

Father in Heaven

Noah, I command you,
go out of the ship at once,
your wife and your children also,
birds, beasts, and every creature.

Noah

Great honour to you, Lord of Heaven.
You help weak and strong
in need, truly, when it is required.

Den in mes, bean ha brase:
Chattall, ethyn ha bestas;
    Myns a ve in lester dres.

An alter redy, veary fayre.

Yn dewhillyans pehosow
Gwethill alter me a vydn.
Me a vidn gwythyll canow,
Ha sacryfice lebmyn
Radn ehan a bub sortowe,
Keffrys bestas hag ethyn,
    Gans hedna thy honora.

Some good church songys to be songe at the alter.

Ha rag hedna gwren ny cana
    In gwerthyans ȝen Tase omma.

And frankensens.

Father in Heaven

Hebma ythew sawer wheake,
Hag in weth sacrifice da.
Pur wyer Noy, ef thybma a blek,
A leyn golan pan ewa
    Thyma ve gwryes.

Rag hedna sure me a wra
Benytha woȝa hebma
    In ybbern y fyth gwelys
A rayne bowe to appeare.

2489-90. *line arrangement as Stokes; after 2486 in MS.*

Let us come out, small and great:
cattle, birds and beasts;
all who were brought into the ship.

An altar ready, very fine.

In atonement for sins
I will prepare an altar.
I will have songs,
and sacrifice now
some of the kind of every species,
both beasts and birds,
to honour you with them.

Some good church songs to be sung at the altar.

And therefore let us sing
here in honour of the Father.

And frankincense.

Father in Heaven

This is a sweet savour,
and a good sacrifice also.
Truly, Noah, it pleases me,
since it is made to me
from a loyal heart.

Therefore surely I shall cause
forever after this
that there will be seen in the sky

A rainbow to appear.

An gabm thavas in teffry.
Pesqwythe mays gwella hy,
Remembra a hanaw why
Me a wra bys venarye,
    Trest ge thybma.

Distructyon vythe an parna
Benytha der thower ny wra,
Wos destrea an bysma.
    Ha rag hedna

Cresowgh, collenwowh keffrys
An noer vyes a dus arta.
Pub ehan ha beast in byes,
Puskas in moer magata,
    A vyth thewgh susten omma.

Nynges tra in bysma gwryes
Mes thewhy a wra service.
Bethowh ware navo lethys
Mabe dean genawhy neb pryes.

Ha mar petha in della,
Me a vidn ye requyrya
A thewla an kethe dean na
Y woose a theffa scullya.
Yn havall thymma obma
Ymadge dean gwrega shapya:
Mar am kerowgh dell gotha
Why a wra orthaf cola.

Noy Ny a vidn gwyll in della, 27r
Del ewa dewar theny,
Ha thethe worthya rag nefra,
Pardellew agen dewty.

2503. gwella hy *this ed;* gwella why hy *MS*.

the rainbow indeed.
Whenever I see it,
I shall always
remember you,
trust in me.

I shall never cause
any destruction by water like that,
so as to destroy this world.
And therefore

increase, also fill
the world with men again.
Every bird and beast in the world,
also the fishes in the sea,
will be food for you here.

There is nothing made in this world
that will not do you service.
Beware that there be no man killed
by you at any time.

And if it should be so,
I shall require it
at the hands of that same man
who should come to spill his blood.
Here in likeness to myself
I shaped the image of man:
if you love me as you should
you will hear me.

Noah We shall do that,
as it is our obligation,
and we shall worship you forever,
as it is our duty.

An kethe jorna ma ew de,
ȝen Tase Dew rebo grassyes.
Why a wellas, pub degre,
Leas matters gwarryes,
    Ha creacion oll an byse.

In weth oll why a wellas
An keth bysma consumys
Der lyvyow a thower pur vras.
Ny ve udn mabe dean sparys,
    Menas Noy, y wreag, hay flehys.

Dewh a vorowe a dermyn:
Why a weall matters pur vras,
Ha redempcion granntys
Der vercy a Thew an Tase,
    Tha sawya neb es kellys.

Mynstrells, grewgh theny peba,
May hallan warbarthe downssya,
    Del ew an vaner han geys.

Heare endeth the Creacion of the Worlde, with Noyes Flude, wryten by William Jordan the 12th of August 1611.

2536. creacion creacon *MS*.
2544. redempcion redempcon *MS*.

[*Turns to audience*] This same day is over,
thanks be to God the Father.
You have seen, every one of you,
many matters played,
and the creation of all the world.

Also you have all seen
the same world consumed
by tremendous floods of water.
Not one human being was spared,
except Noah, his wife, and his children.

Come tomorrow on time:
you will see very great matters,
and redemption granted
through the mercy of God the Father,
to save whoever is lost.

Pipe up for us, minstrels,
that we may dance together,
as is the manner and the custom.

Here ends the Creation of the World, with Noah's Flood, written by William Jordan, 12th August 1611.

COMMENTARY

title. *the first daie* It is not known how many days the whole cycle would have taken (if a continuation ever existed). The *Creacion* covers less than half the biblical history contained in *OM*, and the *Ordinalia* only reaches the Resurrection on the third day. The St. Ives Borough Accounts for 1575 apparently refer to a play lasting six days (see 'Plen an gwary', p. 206); the *Creacion* may be the first day of a cycle of similar length. If it was finished, the Breton cycle would have lasted even longer, for there the death of Noah is not reached until the end of the *second* day.

1 sd. *when he speakethe of Heaven* i.e. at line 23.

the levys The *clowde* seems to have had hinged sections that opened like the leaves of a triptych to reveal God and Heaven inside. Cf. the 'duble clowde' listed in the records of St. Swithin's, Lincoln (see Craig, p. 279). Later God travels from earth to Heaven in a cloud (see 420 sd.); this must have included some kind of mechanical lifting device. For other similar clouds see *Chester*, p. 450, l. 356 sd; 'N-town', p.351, ll. 53-4; York, p. 461, l. 175, and Kolve, p.26.

1. Revelations i 8. All the English creation plays open with this text, though *OM* does not.

4. *agy than clowdes* 1 sd. supports Nance's emendation.

5. Cf. Genesis i 2: 'And the Spirit of God moved upon the face of the waters'.

6-11. God emphasises that 'in the heavens He is not any one person of the Trinity but the Trinity itself' (Woolf, p. 106).

14 ff. As the marginal note at line 12 points out (see collation), the creation of Heaven and earth is described in Genesis i.

19. *worthe compas* Nance (*C-E D* compas) suggested that this idiom meant 'completely' but it is surely to be compared with Old French *par compas:* 'with measure and order' (cf. *OED* compass *sb.*[1] 1: 'Measure, proper proportion, regularity'). Line 19 glosses Wisdom xi 20: 'thou hast ordered all things in measure and number and weight', a popular text in medieval commentaries on the Creation. Cf. 'in mesure god mad alle manere thynges,/And sette hit at a sertayn and at a syker numbre' (*Piers Plowman* (C-text), XXIII, 254-5).

OED points out that the early history of 'compass' is indeterminate: 'measure' and 'pair of compasses' both being early senses. In the iconography of the Creation God is often shown wielding a pair of compasses (see frontispiece; also *Holkham*, fol. 2, pp.56-9 and the first panel of the St. Neot Creation window, plate 2). The motif arises from Proverbs viii, 27: 'When he set a compass upon the face of the depth' (see Antony Blunt, 'Blake's "Ancient of Days"', *Journal of the Warburg Institute*, II (1938-9), pp. 53-63). God 'may well have held such a pair of gigantic compasses' (Woolf, p. 113) in the staging of this scene in the cycle plays. Cf. 'a biglie blese here will I build,/a heaven without endinge,/and caste a comely compasse/by comely creation' (*Chester*, p.2, ll. 38-41). If He did so in the *Creacion* (and the appearance of the compasses in the St. Neot Creation window might confirm this), His division of the angels into 'degrees' (see note on 51) would have been rather apposite.

23 sd. See 1 sd.

26. *joy ha cane* lit. 'joy and song', a hendiadys.

an gorthe 'worship me' - we would expect *am*, but n frequently replaces m in *Creacion*, cf. 333, 396, 659, etc.

27 ff. The Creation of the Angels is dramatised also in *Chester*, 'N-Town', *York*, *VT* and the Breton Creation, but *Chester* and *VT* are the only other versions to name the orders individually. For the development of the tradition through the works of the pseudo-Dionysius, see Skeat's note in *Piers Plowman* Pt. IV i, pp. 33-5.

29. *canhasawe* 'messengers': the literal meaning of 'angels' in the original Greek.

40. *Ty* Singular: each of the nine orders was represented by one angel. This explains the singular forms in 55 and 56 (see also 326 sd.). The angels in the third degree are addressed in the plural, however.

48. Lucifer presided over a tenth, nameless order: 'But criste kingene kynge kniȝted ten,/Cherubyn and seraphin suche seuene and an othre' (*Piers Plowman*, I, 105-6). It was above the other nine (cf. l. 47). When Lucifer fell, mankind was created to replace it (see 242 ff.).

51. 'the second degree' The angels were divided into three hierarchies of three orders each.

55. *Potestas* singular, like *Domynashon* in 56. See note on 40.

73. *asone* Stokes prints *a[s]sone*, but there seems no reason to emend what is clearly an elision.

78 sd. See line 74. God probably descends in his *clowde* (see note on 1 sd.).

81-4. Light was made on the *first* day, as well as the division between day and night, according to Genesis i 3-5.

85. *cudnyke* This is clearly the MS reading, *pace* Stokes, who prints *conduyke*. Cf. Lhuyd, pp. 43, 47, 'kudnick' = *astutus, cautus,* and *gonnycke* (*Creacion* 1404), which Stokes compares in 'CG' to *connyngh* in *PC* 1458, citing Lhuyd.

89-90. This notion of the sea protecting the land from pollution is curiously similar to part of Gaunt's famous speech in *Richard II:* 'This other Eden, demi-paradise,/This fortress built by Nature for herself/Against infection' (II, i, 42-4), especially as the Arden edition compares 'This other Eden' to 'our sea-walled garden' (III, iv, 43).

96. 'abundantly' *pur splan*, lit. 'very splendidly'.

110. 'and every thing that creepeth upon the earth after his kind', Genesis i 25. God's mention of *prevas* in particular is no doubt meant to remind us of the Serpent's role in the Fall.

113 ff. The story of the Fall of the Angels derives from a number of biblical texts. The first full account was in *The City of God* (see Woolf, p. 105).

113. That the first English words in the play are spoken by the Devil is no accident. Most of the snatches of English are spoken by the bad characters, particularly Lucifer, Cain and Lamech. Cf. the use of French for bad characters in the English plays, eg. Herod (*Towneley*, p. 181, ll. 512-3) and his messenger (*Coventry*, pp. 16-17, ll. 475-85). Two of Lucifer's speeches contain several consecutive lines in English (195-9; 276-9). See Intro., p. xxxiv.

124. 'shining like fire' An ironic reminder of Lucifer's fate.

141. Keigwyn notes here 'It is a common expression in Cornwale to call a great man a great polat, perhaps from pol a Head or Top'. In the *Creacion* the word is used only of evil characters (see Intro., p. xxi).

144. Lucifer forgets that God is omniscient.

147 sp. Presumably this angel is of the first degree, as speeches from angels of the second and third degrees follow. Lucifer's order was sometimes thought to be made up of rebel angels from the other nine. Cf. 'Of ich order, in thare degre/ the X part fell downe with me' (*Towneley*, p. 8, ll. 254-7).

155 sp. *in that degree* See note on 147 sp.

165-6. See note on 113.

168-9. Cf. 128 and 130. Lucifer's angel shows his loyalty by repeating his words.

174. *Deform* i.e. 'uncreate', but also literally 'deform', cf. 478.

192-4. But cf. 133-4!

195-99. See note on 113.

195. *of a thought* in an instant (*OED* thought *sb.*[1] 3a).

198. *Semely am* The pronoun 'I' is understood.

202 sd. *the throne* i.e. God's throne.

The Angell i.e. Michael, the leader of the angels, Cf. 975 sd.

203 sp. The first 3 in the *MS* (see collation) seems redundant (cf. 179 sp. and also those for the Angels and Devils in the first and second degrees). However as there *were* three orders in each degree the redactor *may* have meant to be this specific. Either way the speaker is almost certainly Michael the Archangel (these were in the third degree, see 61); see note on 214.

214 ff. In this speech Lucifer scornfully echoes some of Michael's words. Cf. *Ty, Myhall* (214) and *Te, Lucifer* (203); *ythos* (214 and 204); *ortha vy* (215) and *ortha vaker* (204); *dowte* (220) and *dowt* (205); *rag henna* (222 and 205). Unfortunately it is difficult to reproduce this effect in translation (though I have tried).

214. *Myhall* Doubtless Michael the Archangel is meant, though this could simply be an expletive, as in 600.

224-5. Cf. 128-30, 125, and 168-9. Lucifer protests too much.

227 sd. *before Heven* i.e. in front of (the station of) Heaven. God is in the *place* now, having descended after line 78. Cf. *Noy commeth before Heven*, 2243 sd.

227 sp. MS *in heaven* must be an error (see above note).

228. God recalls Lucifer's own words, see 123.

230. *breyf* Obscure. Keigwyn translates 'presently'; Pryce glosses 'brief', Stokes 'soon(?)' - none of these senses seems to fit the context. Nance emends to *braf*, translating 'greatly'.

232-3. God echoes the words of both Michael and Lucifer; see note on 214 ff.

241. *opea* lit. 'thow open', understanding 'to him'.

245 sd. Cf. 'Ugly Hell, gape not ' (*Dr. Faustus*, xix, 189). In both plays the Hell-mouth must have had a contrivance that allowed the jaws to open at appropriate moments, perhaps like that with 'a nether chap' listed among props belonging to the Lincoln corporation (see Anderson, p. 127).

251. *fyne* Stokes and Nance render 'fine'.

271. lit. 'still very proudly falling'. *Trebytchya* is borrowed from Ml. Breton *trebuchaff* 'stumble' (see J.R.F. Piette, *French Loanwords in Middle Breton* (Cardiff, 1973), p. 186). Though resisting, Lucifer is apparently aware that his fall is imminent. A little awkward, but the sense is confirmed by *Creacion* 1580, which is clarified by the stage direction *let hem tomble*, 1564 sd.

272. *Hanter* A gross exaggeration; only a tenth of the angels fell with Lucifer (see note on 147 sp.). But in production it would *seem* to be half, since there is only one good and one bad angel to represent each order.

276-9. See note on 113.

284 ff. God is still speaking from the *place*, in front of Heaven.

291. lit. 'and very frightful villain' (?). There may be corruption here; this does not rhyme with 288 as it should. Stokes prints *byllen[y]* and renders 'and very awful villainy', which Nance follows with 'and most frightful vileness'. Cf., though, *PC*, 41, where [an] *bylen* = 'the devil'.

300 sd. *the rome wher Lucyfer ys* See Intro., p. li.

314 sd. *the trone* i.e. God's throne, cf. 202 sd.

326 sd. *devylls of lether and sprytys on cordys* Probably puppets (see George Speaight, *The History of the English Puppet Theatre* (London, 1955), p. 54). J.W. Robinson ('On the Evidence for Puppets in Late Medieval England', *Theatre Survey*, XIV (1973) pp. 112-117) suggests that *of lether* may mean '[clothed] in leather' rather than 'made of leather', and that *sprytys on cordys* refers to the damned led in ropes by the devils. But (as he says) there *were* no damned souls yet, and the *Creacion* is very precise in its delineation of Hell and Purgatory, so I think this unlikely. One illustration of the Fall of the Angels in the *Speculum humanae salvationis* shows black spidery dangling devils that could easily have been leather puppets (plate 127).

ruining This emendation occurred to me because of Milton's use of the word in connection with *his* fallen angels, as in 'hell saw/Heaven ruining from heaven' (*Paradise Lost*, VI, 867-8). See *OED* ruin *v* II 5 b. The earliest citation is 1604, but the related noun (which Milton also uses frequently, when writing of Satan especially:

Him the almighty power
Hurled headlong flaming from the ethereal sky
With hideous *ruin* and combustion down
To bottomless perdition

(*Paradise Lost*, I, 43-6, cf. also II 305, VI 875)

occurs much earlier - one of its special senses almost seems to be of 'downfall from Heaven', though this is not recorded in *OED*.

'the place' (see Intro., pp. xlix-l).

Nine angells i.e. the nine good angels - each order was represented by one actor, see notes on 40, 272.

327. *Owte, ellas* Common demonic exclamations in the English plays. Cf. 'Out, alas! For woo and wickednesse/I ame so fast bounde' (*Chester*, p. 12, ll. 270-1), 'Owt, owt, what sorrowe is this' (*Chester*, p. 20, l. 161), 'Owte! I dar noȝt loke, allas!' (*York*, p. 183, l. 175). Later used by Cain, 1568, and Lamech's boy, 1705.

'Masks are dropped' lit. 'faces are gone' (cf. Nance 'Braggings are over', comparing *fas* 'boasting', *PC* 2106, *PC* 2110). I think Lucifer is speaking *literally*; cf. *Hager ythof defashes*, 478. When he falls he changes rapidly from angel to devil *apariled fowle*: he probably wore a devil's costume beneath his angel's attire like Lucifer in *Wisdom*, *in a dewyllys aray wythowt and wythin as a prowde galonte* (*Macro*, p. 125).

332. Cf. 'there to dwell/In adamantine chains and penal fire,/Who durst defy the omnipotent to arms' (*Paradise Lost*, I, 47-9). Carey and Fowler compare *Jude* 6 and 2 *Peter* ii 4: 'God spared not the angels that sinned, but... delivered them into chains of darkness'. Cf. also Chaucer's references to 'the cheyne of Sathanas ' (*Lenvoy a Bukton*. 9-10) and 'the serpent depe in helle ybounde' (*Man of Law's Tale*, 361) and Robinson's note on this, p. 694. In a liturgical play of the *Presentation of the Blessed Virgin Mary* performed at Avignon in 1385 Michael leads in Lucifer by an iron chain held in his left hand: *in sinistra manu tenebit quandam cathenam ferream, cum qua Lucifer in collo ligatus retro sequetur Michaelem* (Young, II, p. 230).

333. Cf. 927.

335. After this line about two-thirds of the folio (4v) remain blank.

336 sp. The only Latin speech-heading in the play. God's words in this speech are very close to *OM* 65 ff. and *OM* uses Latin speech-headings throughout. See Intro., p. xxxv ff., and Appendix II.

droke preve God displays his foreknowledge: Lucifer is not *yet* a serpent.

341. *Ebron* Hebron, the modern El-Halil, 23 miles SSW of Jerusalem, was chosen by Abraham as his nomadic home. It contained his tomb, and also those of Isaac and Jacob (see *ODCC*, p. 616).

Owing to a Vulgate mistranslation, Hebron was erroneously believed to be the burial place of Adam also (see *Catholic Encyclopaedia,* VII, pp. 184-6). Thence it was sometimes said to be his birth-place too, e.g. in *Cursor Mundi* 'In a dale he wroght adam/þat ebron hatte, in hebru nam' (p. 30, ll. 405-6).

343 sd. *whytt lether* i.e. to represent nakedness. Cf. the item in the records of the Coventry Smith's company for 1451: 'payed for vj skynnys of whit leder to Godds garment xviijd.' (*Coventry*, p. 85).

the conveyour See Intro., p. lxiii ff.

344 ff. Cf. *OM* 57-72.

348-9. 'And the Lord God... breathed into his nostrils the breath of life; and man became a living soul' (Genesis ii 7).

351. Genesis iii 19: 'for dust thou art, and unto dust thou shalt return', part of God's words to Adam *after* the Fall (as in *Creacion* 952-3).

360 sd. *two fayre trees* 'the tree of life also in the midst of the garden, and the tree of knowledge of good and evil' (Genesis ii 9).

the Tree the Tree of Knowledge (see 377).

a fowntayne The presence of a fountain in Paradise results from a Vulgate mistranslation of the Hebrew *gnedh* in Genesis ii 5 as *fons*, now corrected in the Authorised Version to 'mist' (see Carey and Fowler, p. 623).

363 sd. No doubt the wonders of Paradise were revealed by the drawing of a curtain.

365 sd. How was this done?

370. Cf. *OM* 77.

380. *Ankowe* See note on 984.

390-2. Cf. *OM* 99-101.

392 sd. 1. *by the conveyour* See Intro., p. lxiii ff., and Plate 2, panel 5.

394. Genesis ii 23 'she shall be called woman, because she was taken out of man'.

396. Adam does not name Eve until *after* the Fall in Genesis iii 20. In most of the analogues, following *Cursor Mundi*, he calls her 'virago' here. In *York*, however, both Adam and Eve are named by God, before the Fall (p. 15, l. 44).

397 sd. The fish and animals probably *apeare* on a painted cloth or boards like the animals in the Chester Noah play (see *Chester*, p. 48, 160 sd.).

403 *bashe* see *OED* bash *v.*[1] 2a: 'to be daunted or dismayed'. Without emending *saw*, one might translate 'But do not surpass me in any way' (cf. *a bashe*, 149) but *sav* makes sense of the stage direction.

398-404. Cf. *OM* 117-123.

404 ff. The naming of the animals occurs before the Creation of Eve in *Cursor Mundi* and the English plays, as in Genesis.

405 *chattall* i.e. domestic animals of various kinds, livestock (cf. *OED* chattel *sb.* 3).

409 *ehan* Normally *ethyn* in *Creacion*, but cf. 2514.

409 sd. The idea that the serpent had *a virgyn face* is attributed in the *Historia Scholastica* to Bede, although there seems to be no mention of it in Bede's writings. See Woolf, p. 115, and the article by J.K. Bonnell cited there: also J.B. Trapp, 'The Iconography of the Fall of Man', *Approaches to Paradise Lost*, ed. C.A. Patrides (London, 1968), pp. 223-265. See plate 4. This *fyne serpent made* was probably some sort of puppet, like the *devylls of lether* of 326 sd.; in 488 sd. she *voydeth* when Lucifer tries to enter her (see note on 520 sd.). But she was a costume as well, because Lucifer 'enters' her (see 525 sd., and cf. 'the edders coate I will take one' (*Chester*, p. 21, l. 206), and later 'comes out' of her, leaving her behind in the Tree of Knowledge, after the Fall (see note on 917 sd.).

410. Cf. *OM* 135.

413-20. Cf. *OM* 141-8.

418. A further instance of God's forknowledge: there is no reason yet why man should *need* to be saved.

419. *dowhethyans* Stokes emends to *desquethyans* to conform with the parallel line *OM* 122. But there is no need to assume textual corruption if the reading makes sense. Though *dowhethyans* is a nonce word, the verb *dowethy* is common. The sense 'ending, conclusion' suits the context. Cf. Keigwyn's rendering: 'the latter end'.

420 sd. *in a clowde* See note on 1 sd.

444-5. Cf. 368-9. Lucifer has heard God's words there. Note that he uses the 'English' *warden* where God's speech had *gwethyas*. See note on 113.

459. *omma* 'here' is used for Hell rather than *ena* 'there' as in 423, but I think to emphasise Lucifer's closeness to Hell, rather than to suggest that he is speaking *from* it.

461. *potvan* For justification of Nance's emendation, see Smith, p. 6.

464. Cf. 341-2. Again a Cornish word in God's speech (*le*) is replaced by an 'English' one (*romys*). See note on 113.

481 sp. *Belzabub* 'the prince of the devils', Matthew xii 24. For other references see Carey and Fowler, pp. 466-7.

488 sd. *walke* This reminds us that the pre-lapsarian serpent went upright. See Carey and Fowler, p. 886. (Note the irony of the beautiful serpent's appearing after Beelzebub's comments on Lucifer's ugliness.)

494. *prevent* 'forestall', with a pun on *preve*.

497. *der entent* 'on purpose' - Lucifer is apparently unaware of the irony of this (he will be *fulfilling* God's purpose by using the serpent).

500-1. See note on 409 sd.

502. *Sottall* 'Now the serpent was more subtil than any beast of the field', Genesis iii 1.

505. *prevathe* 'privately'. Probably a double pun, on *preve* like *prevent*, 494, and with sexual innuendo (see note on 520 sd.).

506. *mos* lit. 'go'; 'sneak' is an attempt to make something of the pun on *preve* in 505.

507. Patristic commentaries emphasise that the Serpent could only speak when the Devil took control of her (see e.g. *PL*, XCIII, 229, 275-6). For the contrary belief, that 'Beestes and briddes koude speke and synge' before the Fall, see Robinson, p. 752, note on *Nun's Priest's Tale* 2881.

512 sp. *Torpen* 'Bellyhead'. The name is not spoken, and does not occur elsewhere. Descriptive of the demon's looks?

518. See note on 113.

520 sd. In view of *gorta*, 'stop' in 522, Lucifer is probably the subject of *stayeth* as of *ofereth* (the omission of the subject pronoun is quite common in English of this period, cf. 198) rather than the Serpent. The object 'her' is understood from the end of the sentence. 'It is difficult to imagine how this scene was staged, unless the Serpent dress was first agitated on the end of a pole by some hidden stage hand' (Anderson, pp. 143-4). There must surely have been some sexual by-play involved - Lucifer could be getting on the costume while pretending to struggle with the Serpent, and there is probably innuendo in 523.

521. *Re deball dowethy* lit. 'May you come to a bad end'.

525 sd. See note on 409 sd.

530-1. Lucifer (the Serpent) now begins to speak more sweetly, so that Eve takes him for an angel (see note on 566-7).

536. *gycke* Cf. R. Hemon, *Geriadur Istorel ar Brezhoneg* ['Historical Dictionary of Breton'] (Paris, 1958-date), part 11 (1965), pp. 1073-4 *grik*, ?*gwik*: '(ne disant) mot, chut' (quoting two middle Breton texts with *guic, guyc*).

537. *mycke* Cf. Hemon, *op. cit.* part 23 (1973), p. 2233, *mik* (3) 'chut! silence!' (4) *hep ober mik na man* 'without attracting the least attention (sans porter la moindre attention).

544-6. Cf. *OM* 149-51.

549 sd. *when she speaketh* Probably *she* = Eve (as in 552 sd.), though it could be the Serpent since 'its' speaking *was* a wonder, cf. 507. (The Serpent is female, though 'Lucifer the Serpent' is masculine).

550. *troes ha cane* lit. 'noise and song', a hendiadys.

561-2. lit. 'Do not take wonder from it, nor [take] any fear that there is seeing me'.

564. Eve's words show how right Lucifer was to assume that the Serpent's appearance would please her (see 526-8).

565. *whath* 'yet', a nice irony.

dowt Stokes and Nance both render 'doubt', but the sense 'fear' seems more suitable here.

566-7. Eve assumes from Lucifer's assurance that he has come 'hastily from Heaven' that he is an angel, as she later tells Adam (see 760). Here, as in 'N-town' and the Norwich Play, the playwright seems to be following the apocryphal tradition that the devil when tempting took the form of an angel of light (see Woolf, p. 117). 'From the dramatic point of view the value of this apocryphal fantasy is that it allows the tempter to proceed in a more elevated and therefore deceptive manner; he does not have to approach the issue by cunning questioning, but... he greets Eve as though she were a noble lady from the world of romance' (*ibid.*).

581. *meare tha volta* Translation uncertain. I follow the suggestion of Cuillandre (*RC* XLIX, p. 126) that the construction is to be compared to *mer tha vlamya*, 161, and means 'greatly to speak boldly', but with some misgivings.

584. *da cotha; yw* lit. 'Good it ought [to be]; it is'. The infinitive normally occurs after *coth(a)* but the MS reading makes sense if we think of Lucifer speaking *cotha* in an undertone in his 'own' voice, thinking of the benefit to himself in the transaction. This double sense is continued in 586.

586. *fyllall* lit. 'fail'; Lucifer means 'fail (to succeed in my design)', as well as 'do wrong', though Eve is only aware of the latter meaning.

596. *os ehan* Cf. *dres ehan*, 362, lit. 'beyond kind', i.e. 'beyond everything'. Here *os* (= *a wos*) *ehan* probably means 'for the sake of everything', i.e. 'at all costs'.

597-8. This is the Serpent's reiterated temptation, cf; 622-3, 643-4, 697-8. Its success with Eve is shown by the fact that she uses similar words to Adam, see 782-3.

600. *Myhall* Another irony, Michael having been instrumental in sending Lucifer to Hell.

603. Cf. 590. Eve has quickly changed her tune.

607. *re sent* 'by saint'. Perhaps Eve is still thinking of Michael, as in 600.

608. *rowlya* Stokes's emendation seems right in view of the similarity between some forms of l and t in the MS, although *rowtya* (MS) occurs once elsewhere, in Gwavas f. 101 v, as the equivalent of 'dominabitur' in Genesis iii 16.

615. Cf. 453. Eve unconsciously echoes Lucifer's words.

617-8. lit. 'Tell me before resting [immediately],/ I beg you, the news'.

619. Cf. 595.

632. *thesan* an odd form; the initial 'th' is unexplained.

637-8. A serpent's hiss is suggested by the many sibilants in these lines.

651. *men tha gesky* See Cuillandre, *RC*, XLVIII, p. 34, who offers the translation 'te presser fortement'. Alternatively Nance, *C-E D*, *men* ('strong', 'able') offers the translation 'capable of advising thee'.

658. *a rose* One would expect the subject *ef* here. Nance emends to *y rose*. Cf. note on 520 sd. - perhaps this English habit influenced the Cornish?

681. Cf. 485. Lucifer refers to his *own vyadge*, rather than, as Eve thinks, hers.

685-6. lit. 'Adam, truly above everyone/I love him...'.

688-9. In *OM* Eve asks the Serpent to bow down the branch so that she can pick the apple. Here *he* gives the orders.

692. lit. 'since there is need to taste of it'.

700. This is the Serpent's second declaration of love, cf. 670.

706-7. Although Eve says she has no hesitation in tasting the apple, it is not clear that she tastes it at all - the stage directions do not mention it, and Adam implies later that only *he* 'tasted' the apple, see note on 880-1. However, Genesis iii 6 states that Eve ate the fruit before Adam, and she does so in the English plays, so possibly she takes a bite after 707.

724-6. The Serpent might call after Eve as she is leaving, but more probably these lines are spoken after she is out of earshot.'Lucifer the Serpent' remains in the Tree of Knowledge until God's curse after the Fall, and our attention switches to the dialogue between Adam and Eve in a 'different part' of Paradise. Lucifer thinks that Adam and Eve are to 'see him again' in Hell; in fact they go to Limbo.

728. Cf. 637. Eve echoes the Serpent.

738. *gay a avall* lit. 'fine of an apple' is an idiom (cf. *OM* 753, 2441), so Stokes's emendation (*gaya avall*) is not required.

758. The following speech is a close echo of its counterpart in *OM* (213 ff.). See Appendix II.

760. See note on 566-7.

770. *Droke polat* See note on 141.

771. Cf. *OM* 224.

782-3. See note on 597-8.

803. *perill* This is in fact the third time Eve has used the word in six lines, and she obviously *is* afraid of 'peril'. But it seems unsatisfactory to use the word in translating the first two instances (= 'danger').

coynt This can have various meanings. Eve uses it as a term of praise: 'cleverly, skilfully', but it also means 'cunningly'. Cf. *OED* quaint *a.*

804. *horsen kam* 'crooked whoreson' (not easy to render in Modern English).

816. Eve has not spoken of the Serpent, only of the angel she took Lucifer to be. Presumably Adam can see Lucifer the Serpent in the Tree and knows he is evil.

831. *avallowe* Eve seems to have brought back more than one apple, cf. 944.

836. Keigwyn remarks here: 'How well do her daughters imitate her to this day - and her sons, Adam!'

842-4. Cf. *OM* 246-8.

849. 'take and eat' The echo of the communion service can hardly be accidental.

850 sd. There is no mention of Eve tasting the apple. See note on 706.

851-5. Cf. *OM* 249-53.

859 ff. Cf. *OM* 255 ff. (parallels for the rest of this 'scene', see Appendix II).

865 sd. *spekethe every thing* 'says it all', i.e. what she thinks of Adam naked, also indicated by her cold expression (see *OED* strangely adv. 1). (Unless we are to understand that 'he', Adam, is the subject of *spekethe.)*

866 ff. This scene follows Genesis iii 9 ff. fairly closely.

882-3. lit. 'in sweat of labour to eat/you will do until the end'.

901. God does not ask the Serpent this question in Genesis, and obviously He knows the answer. The purpose of the exchange is to bring the message home to the audience.

916. *crushya* a conjectural emendation. What is needed is a word with the sense 'bruise' of Genesis iii 15.

917 sd. See note on 409 sd. The Serpent remains in the tree because it is to be part of Seth's vision of Paradise. See 1772 sd., 1804 sd.

918. lit. 'that I may sing alas', a common way of expressing misery in Cornish, cf. *OM* 308-10.

927. Cf. 333.

938. 'the Oil of Mercy' Christ, the Saviour who will redeem mankind. When Seth visits Paradise to obtain the Oil of Mercy he is given three seeds from the Tree of Life, from which there will grow a tree (the cross) that will eventually bear the Oil of Mercy, the Saviour. This legend

is central to the *Ordinalia* but seems less important in the *Creacion*. Only passing references to the Oil of Mercy occur in the English cycles. The most recent work on the legend is that of Esther C. Quinn, *The Quest of Seth* (Chicago, 1962).

943-53. Genesis iii 17-19.

944. *frutes* See note on 831.

946. The subject 'the ground' is understood, as it occurs in the next line, and it is not necessary to insert a line in which God specifically states his intention of cursing the ground (as Nance does), for we see Him doing it.

966-8. 'Frequently it is by changing the characters' costume that the author impresses his moral meaning on the audience' (T.W. Craik, *The Tudor Interlude* (Leicester, 1962), p. 73). Here again *Creacion* resembles the moral plays - more is made of Adam and Eve's nakedness than their garments in most of the analogues.

927 sp. Apparently singular, as in line 40, although Genesis iii 24 has 'he placed at the east of the garden of Eden Cherubims'. This Cherub does not seem to have come down from Heaven, for only one angel is mentioned in the sd.

975 sd. *the Angell* Presumably Michael, who has brought the clothes from Heaven following God's orders (966-8), although the Cherub is speaking, and he produces the tools for work (981-3), which could not, of course, have come from Heaven.

983 sd. 1. *them* Michael and the Cherub.

sd. 2. *spade* See 981, and cf. the props for the Cappers guild of Coventry: 'Adam's spade and Eve's destaffe' (quoted in Anderson, p. 176). Adam and Eve also appear with a spade and distaff in the St. Neot Creation Window (see plate 2, panel 9).

986. 'Death' Although the figure has his Cornish name, Ankow, there is little else Celtic about him. He conforms to the character familiar from the English moral plays: subservient to God, attacking covetousness, armed with a dart. Cf. 'He that loueth rychesse I wyll stryke with my darte' (*Everyman*, l. 76). He appears here to personify Genesis ii 17: 'in the day that thou eatest thereof thou shalt surely die'. None of

the earlier cycle plays have Death enter at this point, though the Breton Creation does. The Dance of Death may have influenced the scene: an interesting analogue is to be found in the Lyons Dance of Death woodcuts (attributed to Holbein), the third of which shows Adam and Eve being driven from Paradise by an angel with a sword of fire, accompanied by Death playing on a beggar's lyre. Death's opening words closely resemble those of his counterpart in the 'N-town' 'Death of Herod': 'I am dethe goddys masangere' (p. 174, 1. 177). Does his description of himself as a 'messenger' imply that he is meant to be an angel? See note on 29.

998. Cf. 445.

1014. *kyny* See note on 918.

1015. The object 'him' is the Serpent: Eve is still reflecting on Death's last words.

1029. *dyckles* Obscure. My translation follows Nance, who renders 'without refuge' (printing *dyclos*).

1044. Mankind was vegetarian before the Flood (see note on 1468 ff.).

1054 ff. The ultimate source for the Cain and Abel story is Genesis iv 1-16.

1061-2. lit. 'a service to a charge and its fellow/to control corn, and cattle'. MS *teag* is obviously corrupt; for my emendation cf. 1063. Nance prints *service dhe'n yl* and translates 'Service for the one and the other'.

1067. *war,* 'over' Adam is still thinking of Abel's 'charge' over the animals from which he is to make his offering.

1070. *Mount Tabor* There is no mention of the place of sacrifice in Genesis, nor even that it is a mountain, though reference is made to 'this hill' e.g. in *Towneley* (see Cawley, p. 5, 1. 170). In *OM* God tells Adam that Mount Tabor is where the tithes must be laid (and later the dying Moses plants his rods there for David to find). Perhaps, because it was acknowledged as the scene of Christ's Transfiguration (see *Catholic Encyclopaedia*, XIV, p. 552), it was considered to be a suitable place for sacrifice.

1077. Cf. *OM* 683, where the line is spoken by Adam just before he sends Seth to Paradise.

1087. The plural 'fruits' is retained here since crops in general are meant.

1091. The St. Neot Creation window depicts Cain's 'bush of smoke' blowing downwards into his face, while Abel's smoke rises, showing that God has accepted it (see plate 2, panel 10). For the tradition see Anderson, p. 144; Emerson, p. 848.) Cain later hides in a bush, ironically. See note on 1542 sd.

1097. Note the irony.

1107. This seems a suitable point for God's descent. He returned to Heaven at 953, and must be in the place again by 1142.

1115. 'on the jaw' perhaps this seemed appropriate because of the use of a jawbone as weapon - it would be easier to kill Abel by hitting him over the head, as shown e.g. in the St. Neot Creation window (see plate 2, panel 11). In *OM* 540 the blow is also *war an challa* although the accompanying sd. reads *Tunc percuciet eum in capite*. But see 1112. For the jawbone motif see Emerson, pp. 853-4; who traces it back to the ninth century *Solomon and Saturn*. It appears to be confined to the English (and Cornish) versions. See further J.K. Bonnell, 'Cain's Jawbone', *PMLA* XXXIX (1924), pp. 140-5; M. Schapiro, 'Cain's Jawbone that did the First Murder', *Art Bulletin* XXIV (1942), pp. 205-212.

1124. See note on 113.

1129. Cf. 440.

1142 sd. *hem* i.e. Cain, cf. 1164 sd.

1142-6. 'And the Lord said unto Cain, Where is Abel thy brother? And he said, I know not: Am I my brother's keeper?' (Genesis iv, 9).

1142. Cf. *OM* 571.

1150-1. i.e. 'Are you suggesting he's incapable of looking after himself?' But Stokes and Nance take 1151 as modifying 1152: 'when he cannot look after himself I would not be his servant'.

1153-9. Cf. *OM* 577-83 (parallels intermittently throughout this section; see Appendix II).

1153. *voice* In the parallel line *OM* 577 *voys* was translated 'blood' by Norris: 'Behold the blood of dead Abel'. Phyllis Harris follows this with 'Behold the blood of the death of Abel' (see the discussion in *OMN*, pp. 342-3). But Nance renders *OM* 577 'Behold the voice of the death of Abel', which seems correct in view of the stage direction *vox clamat* (*OM* 577 sd.), as well as because the spelling should be *woys*, if the Cornish word meaning 'blood' is intended. In Genesis iv 10 'the voice of thy brother's blood crieth unto me from the ground.'

1167 ff. Cain commits the ultimate sin of Despair:'wanhope, that makyth a man noght to trusten in goddys mercy; for hym thynketh his synne is so myche, that he may neuere haue forgivenesse' (*Jacob's Well*, ed. A. Brandeis (London, EETS, 1890), p.112).

1178. Cf. Genesis iv 15.

1179 sd. Genesis does not specify the type of mark, but it is said to be a pair of horns in some Jewish sources (see Emerson, pp. 868-9). The use of *omega* seems to be unique. Cain as the first murderer is also the worst and therefore 'the last'. Nb. the *marcke* omega (ω) would resemble horns when placed on Cain's forehead. See 1371.

1193. Stokes assumes *rogella* to be a corruption of *rug kelas*, translating 'if he have hidden(?) his brother'. I follow this but take *ye vrodar* as subject. Cain refers (aside) to having hidden Abel in a ditch (see 1136 sd., 1125-6). Nance, however, rejects the MS reading and prints *na wovyn orth y vroder*, 'ask it not of his brother'.

1194-5. Ironically, Cain's dismissal of Abel is descriptive of his own later plight. He, not Abel, wanders off like a hobgoblin, for which he is taken by Lamech's servant (see 1587). For *bucka* and *bucka noos* see P.L. Henry, 'The Goblin Group', *ÉC* VIII (1958-9), p. 406.

1208. This line is also dependent on *ny berraf* (1207). See Smith, p.3.

1219 sd. *profer* subjunctive, as often in stage directions (cf. *e.g.* 1181 sd.).

1245. *Na sor*. Adam echoes Eve in 1233.

1285. Cf. 1274.

1290. Stokes translates 'begone, mother', but *dama* seems more likely to refer to Cain's wife (cf. *OED* dame *sb.* 2) in view of the sd. Nance moves the line to follow 1286, printing *Avoydyama!* and translating 'I will be off'.

1295 sp. Genesis does not reveal the name of Cain's wife. It is given as Chalmana in the *Historia Scholastica* (*PL* CXCVIII, 1076). She does not appear in the English cycles, but is present in the *VT*, along with her (and Cain's other) sisters, Delbora and Noema.

1303. *Tety valy* Cf. *OED* tilly-vally: 'fiddlesticks!', apparently first used by Skelton. Origin unknown. Anderson relates it to Titivillus, the name of the devil who collects whispers in his sack (see pp. 176-7). Cf. 2379.

1306. *gwella tha geare* cf. *gvella the cher*: 'improve thy spirits' (*OM* 166).

1335-6. This is the second reference to Cain's incest, cf. 1298-9. Of course he had no choice but to marry his sister.

1364-5. Cf. 1167 ff., and see note.

1371. The 'horn' of Cain's forehead: both his 'brow' and his 'mark' (of horns), see note on 1179 sd.

1373. God did not actually say 'these very words'; cf. 1176-8. How did Calmana know what God said anyway?

1376. *plague* Stokes and Nance took this to be a variant spelling of *plek*, translating that *seyth plague* 'sevenfold'. This was certainly God's meaning, cf. 1178, where he uses *seyth kymmys*: 'seven times as much'(Genesis iv 15). But Calmana may have misunderstood God and, being connected with evil through Cain, she tends to use more 'English' words. In 1657, and 2346, *plage* clearly means 'punishment'; here Calmana seems literally to mean 'seven plagues'. See also 1613-4.

1383. In Genesis Cain has no children until after he is banished into the land of Nod, when he begets Enoch (Genesis iv 17), Lamech's ancestor. (See Appendix III). No daughter is mentioned there.

1390. See note on 113. Calmana's use of English implies that she is tainted with Cain's evil, cf. note on 1376.

1392 ff. The birth of Seth is recorded in Genesis v 3. For the development of the Seth legend, see note on 938.

1429 sp. *in tent* See Intro., pp. liv-lv.

1429 ff. The following episode apparently originates in the *Historia Scholastica*, PL CXCVIII 1079-80, having been developed to explain Genesis iv, 23-4. It occurs briefly in 'N-town'(but in no other English version) and in the *VT* (4566-4969), where Lamech's assistant is his son Tubalcain, not his servant. It is illustrated in the thirteenth panel of the St. Neot Creation window (see plate 2).

1431. This is the most likely moment for Lamech to come out of his tent.

1432 ff. 'And unto Enoch was born Irad: and Irad begat Mehujael: and Mehujael begat Methusael: and Methusael begat Lamech' (Genesis iv 18). Nb. there is *another* Lamech, father of Noah, and son of Methusaleh, mentioned in Genesis v 25 ff., apparently blameless, and not to be confused with the present character, though one wonders how it was possible to avoid confusion, as with the name of Methusael/Methusaleh here. See note on 2233, and Appendix III.

1435. Lamech is actually of the seventh degree or generation from *Adam*, not Cain (see Appendix III).

1439. *Drog polat* This associates Lamech with Lucifer, see Intro., p. xxi. Note the number of 'English' words in Lamech's speech (see note on 113).

1452. Lamech's two wives were Adah, mother of Jubal (here Tubal) and Jabel, and Zillah, mother of Tubalcain (Genesis iv 19-22).

1459. Lamech's blindness would have been seen as a deserved punishment for his lechery.

1463. Lamech appears to have forgotten about his young ladies.

1464. Lamech's skill in archery would have had especial interest for a Cornish audience, for 'amongst bodily pastimes, shooting carrieth the preeminence' (Carew, p. 72).

1468. 'Hitherto' translation following Nance.

1468 ff. It was generally held that men were vegetarian before the Flood, though there were opponents of this view, such as Procopius (see Allen, p.73).

1487. Cf. 539. Lamech's echo of Eve's words warns us that evil is on its way.

1499-1500. Cf. 789.

1505-6. In his changed, hairy appearance Cain resembles the wodewose or 'wild man of the woods', who in folk plays underwent a ritual killing by an archer. See R. Bernheimer, *Wild Men in the Middle Ages* (Cambridge, Mass., 1962), esp. pp. 52-3 and plates 14 and 16.

1524. Cf. 271, 927 and see Intro., p. xxi, note 7.

1542 sd. *a bush casu* [Lamech] *interfecit Cain inter fructeta* (*Historia Scholastica, PL* CXCVIII, 1079). Cf. 'vndyr ȝon grett busche mayster A best do I se' ('N-town', p. 40, l.166); 'en ce buisson obscur me voiz getter' (*VT* 4686). A nice irony that this is where Cain's 'huge bush of smoke' (1091) has brought him.

1545. *Hans* Henry Lewis (*ÉC* 1, pp. 322-3) suggested emending to *hanys* 'secretly. But cf. *in hans*, 1742.

1551. *seth* 'arrow', possibly reminding the audience of Seth whose goodness counteracts Lamech's evil.

1553 sd. Lamech must be the subject of *shote*, for it is he who kills Cain, i.e. *let his man level the arrow, and then* [*let him*] *shoot*.

1568. *Owt, aylas* Cf. 327, and see note.

1580. *ow trebytchya* Cf. 271 (another link between Cain and the Devil).

1601. *cabm* 'crooked, bent', puns on *Cayme*, 'Cain'.

1613-4. See note on 1376.

1625 ff. Cain's mark - his horns - must be very obvious, and considerable comedy arises from Lamech's behaviour here. He is only partially blind, and is too cowardly to admit to having seen the mark, hoping to avoid punishment.

1646. *dewlaga* 'eyes'; Nance prints *dywla-jy* and translates 'even by thy own hands now', but 'at [in front of] your eyes' is nicely ironic in view of Lamech's 'blindness' (see note on 1625). See also next line.

1647. So Lamech can see to this extent! See also 1700.

1663. Stokes and Nance take this line to modify *wrugaf tha wellas* (1661): 'I didn't see you... because you are deformed'.

1678. Cf. 1266.

1690 ff. Cain persists in his despair. See note on 1167 ff.

1700. Cf. 1647.

1704 sd. *a staff* Probably this was helping Lamech to get about, in his blindness.

1705. Cf. 1568. The boy's repetition of Cain's words, and especially his use of devilish expletives (see note on 327) suggest that he is wicked, so we can be easy in our minds when he is taken by the devils to Hell.

1707. It is difficult to imagine what stage effect could be used to enable the audience to 'see' the boy's head broken in two.

1714. See note on 1705.

1720. *drog lawan* translation following Nance.

1724-5. The first Devil is unaware of the possibilities of Redemption that will be available when the Oil of Mercy, whose seeds are obtained in the next scene, has come to fruition.

1729. *squyth A dev ker assoma squyth* is Adam's exclamation in *OM* 684, the opening of the parallel episode there.

1746 ff. The tradition of the burnt footprints appears to derive from the version of the Seth story in the 13th century Latin *Legende*, and is common in the analogues (see Quinn, pp. 108-9). How would this have been staged?

1749. The earth was cursed in God's speech at 942 ff.

1756 sd. *An Angell* The Cherub, see note on 972 sp.

1772 sd. This appears as two separate directions in the MS: *A tree in Paradice with a meyd in the topp, and reching in her arms the Serpent* (bottom margin, 19r) *the tree wher she was before and Cayne in Hell sorowing and crying* (top margin, 19v). As they stand they are puzzling (why should the *meyd* be *reching* the Serpent, and how can she when they are in different trees?) and they make perfect sense read continuously, taking into account the virgule in the MS after *topp*. They may have been separated by the scribe's running out of space on 19r.

The first tree is the Tree of Life, with the Virgin Mary in the top, the second the Tree of Knowledge (always '*the* Tree', cf. 359 sd. etc.). For *armes* = 'branches' see *OED* arm sb^1 7 - common in early English; for *reching* see *OED* reach *v*^{1} 14). The Serpent was left in the Tree of Knowledge at 916 sd. This is a clear example of a stage-manager's direction to prepare for the authorial direction at 1804. The two trees must be in position in Paradise before Seth gets there.

1781 lit. 'by Adam my father to you' - 'sent' has to be understood unless we follow Nance and change *devethis* (1780) to *danvenys* = sent.

1783 sp. This is the same Cherub that spoke at 972. Elsewhere (1756 sd., 1797 sp.) he is called simply *Angell*.

1792. Seth recalls Adam's words at 1729.

1795. Perhaps the remark that Adam is 'continually crying out' for the Oil of Mercy is intended to contrast him with his son Cain 'sorrowing and crying' in Hell (1772 sd.).

1802 ff. In *OM* Seth is given three separate visions of Paradise: the garden with the fountain and the dry tree; the serpent in the dry tree, and the child in the green tree. These visions correspond closely with the traditional version of the Seth legend, following the Latin *Legende* (see Quinn, pp. 105-127) except that *OM* uses only one tree. In reverting to *two* trees the redactor of the *Creacion* is closer to the earlier form of the legend (and of course to Genesis ii 9) but his placing of Mary in the Tree of Life and Cain (rather than Abel as in the *Legende*) in Hell seems idiosyncratic, as is his combining of the three visions into one.

The Tree of Life was sometimes thought to symbolise the Virgin Mother (see Quinn, pp. 124-5) which may account for the placing of Mary in it. The *meyd* makes a fine contrast with the Serpent *with a virgyn face*. The substitution of Cain for Abel in Hell pit is part of the teaching about the *mansyons* of Hell in this play (see note on 2020 ff.), for Abel's soul would remain in Limbo.

1838. As Seth is a type of Christ the resemblance is perfectly appropriate.

1844. As the sd. indicates, the Angel does not actually bring the apple: he *breaketh it* (breaks it open) takes out three of the pips and brings them (*coore* normally means 'the centre of the pulp... containing the seeds' (*OED*), but here and in 1879 sd. it must mean the seed itself).

1852-4. In *OM* (826-8) Seth is told to place the pips between Adam's teeth and his tongue, and *three* trees will grow from them.

1915. 'more than a hundred years' See note on 1977.

1947 ff. These words are directed to the audience as well as to Seth.

1975. Cf. 2007 (an echo of *OM*).

1977-8. 'And all the days that Adam lived were nine hundred and thirty years: and he died' (Genesis, v, 5).

1980. The number of Adam's children is not given in Genesis. In the *Historia Scholastica* he is said to have had *thirty* sons and daughters besides Cain and Abel (*PL* CXCVIII, 1080); this is followed in e.g. *Cursor Mundi* (pp.78-9). Probably the figure of 32 was arrived at by including Cain and Abel in the number.

1989-2. Cf. 1318-9.

1997. Cf. *OM* 1604, 1703 (words spoken by Aron and Pharaoh).

1999 sd. *a bead* Adam's 'death-bed' probably has a dramatic function as well as a symbolic one. Cf. the direction in *The Castle of Perseverance* that the soul must 'lye under þe bed tyl he schal ryse & playe' (*Macro*, frontispiece). Perhaps something similar took place here, for it is only Adam's *soole* that is taken to Limbo. His body would remain on the bed (and presumably be wheeled out with it). Cf. for example the depiction of the death of Thomas à Becket on the Limoges enamel casket sold at Sothebys on December 13th, 1979. 'On the lid is his body being buried [in a fine tomb] and his soul being carried to heaven by the angels' (*Guardian*, December 14th, 1979). Adam is shown in bed in the St. Neot Creation window, with Seth offering him the pips (see plate 5).

2004. Repeats 1992.

2005-7. Cf. *OM* 850-2.

2007. Cf. 1976.

2008. A virgule in *MS* after henna suggests this is perhaps meant to be two two-stress lines. But I follow Stokes' decision to print as one line, since there is still rhyme.

2013. *than gegen* For Hell as a kitchen see Intro., p. lii , and plate 6.

2020 ff. Hell appears to have two levels or *mansyons*, the *clowster* (Limbo) up above and the *pytt* below (see Intro., p.lii).

2036 sp. This 'third devil' is similar to the third murderer in Macbeth: he only appears here and this is his only speech.

2042 ff. Lucifer's information here, of course, is really for the benefit of the audience.

2071 sd. See note on 1999 sd. It would be easier for the Angel if the soul were played by a small boy (and souls are always depicted as tiny humans in iconography).

2073. 'A place' In Limbo, see note on 2020 ff.

2084-6. Genesis iii 19. Cf. 952-3.

2095 ff. The tradition of the translation of Enoch developed from Genesis v 24: 'And Enoch walked with God: and he was not; for God took him'. It was the subject of the apocryphal *Book of the Secrets of Enoch* (trans. W.A. Morfill, Oxford, 1896). *VT* has the only other extant dramatisation of the episode, though it is mentioned briefly in *RD* (197-9) and *Chester* (p. 335) when Enoch is present at the Harrowing of Hell.

2097 ff. Enoch is descended from Seth, and is great-grandfather of Noah. See Appendix III.

2102 ff. 'And all the days of Enoch were three hundred sixty and five years' (Genesis v 23).

2122 sd. Some kind of mechanical device was probably used here. Cf. *VT*, 1, 210 where Enoch is taken to Paradise *par ung engin subtill*.

2162. For the planetary conjunction that was thought to have caused the Flood, see *Troilus and Criseyde*, III, 624, and Robinson's note, p. 824.

2171. *voydya* Cf. *OED*, void v 3b: 'To deprive of efficacy'.

2172 ff. For the books, see note on 2181 ff.

2181 ff. The ultimate source for the making of the pillars appears to be Josephus I, as reported in the *Historia Scholastica* (*PL* CXCVIII, 1079), where Tubal constructs the pillars. In the *VT*, the only other extant dramatisation of the episode, he is assisted by Jubal. In the *Vita Adae et Evae*, however, the job is done by Seth. The *Creacion* seems idiosyncratic in having Seth and Jared make the pillars (obviously done because two actors were needed for lifting the pillars, but Tubal(cain) and Jabel are bad characters in this play). The notion of making a *historical* record to survive the Flood is also pecular to this play. The original idea was to make a record of the arts and scenes learnt, which was to be written directly on to the pillars (*ne periret ars inventa, scripsit eam in duabus columnis*). The only extant analogue in which books are inserted into the pillars is in Trevisa's translation of Higden's *Polychronicon*: 'bookes þat þey hadde i-made by grete trauaille and studie þey closede hem in tweie greet pileres' which 'translates' *studia sua et artes quas excogitaverant scripserunt in duabus columnis* (*Polychronicon Ranulphi Higden Monachi Cestrensis etc.*, ed. Churchill Babington (Rolls Series, London, 1869) Vol. II, pp. 232-3). Trevisa being a Cornishman, it is possible that he had seen this episode performed in an earlier version of the *Creacion* (i.e. my postulated 'uhr-cycle', see Intro., p. xlvii). In the *VT* the pillars are to be filled 'de plusiers chose' (I, p. 225) - books are not specified.

2193 sp. *Jared* The father of Enoch. See Appendix III.

2198-9. lit. 'of every sort of all books/equally in them in put'. *Egwall* must be used adverbially; it cannot be a noun 'copy' as Nance thought (at least according to *OED*). The translation 'An equivalent amount of every variety of all books is put in each of them' would do less violence to the Cornish, but does not seem possible.

2202. *In diffrans* because one pillar is of brick and one of marble, *kehavall* because each pillar contained the same information in its two books. The 'plan' (2202) was that one of the pillars would survive the destruction, whether by fire or flood.

2207 ff. Note the ironic juxtaposition of Seth's prayer with God's words immediately following. Seth is partly speaking to the audience, of course.

2212 ff. The Noah episode derives ultimately from Genesis vi-x. God's speech is almost identical with *OM* 917-932, except that 2225 and 2230 are added as tail-rhymes. (See Appendix II.) His reference back to the Fall helps stress the continuity of events (in *Towneley* this is done by Noah).

2212. 'And it repeated the Lord that he had made man on earth' (Genesis vi 6).

2213. *preshyous* (1) held in high esteem; (2) extremely.

2215. 'the place' Paradise.

2219. *an eall* 'the angel' Michael, see 963 ff.

2220-1. i.e. because Death was created as a result of the Fall.

2233. 'Lamech' A descendant of Seth, and not to be confused with the Lamech (son of Cain) who appears in the play. See Appendix III and note on 1432 ff.

2236 ff. Noah is not usually portrayed as a man of means; rather the emphasis is on his being hard up. E.g.: 'For I have neither ruff nor ryff,/Spyer, sprund, sprout, nor sprot' (*The Newcastle play*, 83-4, in *Non-Cycle Plays*, p. 28).

2245 ff. Again, almost identical with *OM* 941-64. See Appendix II.

2247-8. Cf. Genesis vi 14.

2251. 'shortly' Stokes translated *a vear spyes* 'of long duration', assuming *vear* to be a mutation of *mear(e)*, 'great, rather than *be(a)r*, 'short'.

2254 sd. This elaborate direction indicates that considerable verisimilitude was aimed at in the construction of the Ark. Like that of the Wakefield version, it was modelled on a contemporary ship (see *Cawley*, p. 97). It was probably assembled from prepared sections (see Woolf, p. 376), as in the Piran Round production of *OM* (see plate 7). The Cornish audience would be very interested in this part of the play. See Nance, 'Shipping and the Cornish Miracle Plays', unpublished lecture in the *Nance Bequest*, Museum of the Royal Institution of Cornwall, Truro.

beam 'One of the horizontal transverse timbers, stretching from side to side of a ship, supporting the deck, and holding the vessel together' (*OED* sb.[1] 15 (1627)).

2255-68. Cf. Genesis vi 14-15, where God also requires a window to be made, says that the door is to be in the *side*, and that the Ark must have three storeys.

2269-70. Unclear. In Genesis God does not ask for joists, and there is no equivalent in any analogue except *OM*, where the lines are also unclear. The problem is that *degys* may mean 'opened' or 'closed', depending on whether *de* represents the negative prefix or the intensifier. Also *dretha* is puzzling: one would expect the strengthening beams to be put *behind* the door, not 'through it'. It is interesting that the playwright (or scribe) wrote *playne* (see collation) for *place*. He may have been looking back to the *planckes playnyes* (2257), or else thinking of the Cornish noun *playne* (or *plen*), the equivalent of English *place* when a technical term for the playing-area (see Intro., p. xlix, note 23).

2271-4. Cf. Genesis vi 19.

2275-7. Cf. Genesis vi 21.

2279-80. 'It is necessary... to remember that the last time God had made a specific command he had been disobeyed' (Woolf, p. 133).

2280. *so mot y go* lit. 'as I may live' (see *OED* go *v.* 1c).

2281-2. This might be a reference to Noah's unsuitability to the task of building the Ark, being 600 years old, of which much is made in some of the English versions, notably 'N-town'.

2287 ff. Japheth would certainly accompany Noah's other sons, though he does not speak here. In most versons Noah builds the Ark alone, though in *Chester* he is helped by the entire family, including all the wives.

2289. *gwyres* lit. 'done'. Nance suggested that *glaw*, 'rain', should be understood here, so that it means 'rained' (*gul glaw* is an idiom like Fr. *faire beau*, cf. 2460). Presumably ironic: Shem has not heard God say that there is to be a flood. But it also emphasises his sense of duty: Noah's sons help their father without asking the reason for his work.

2294. 'in evidence' See 2254 sd.

2295 sp. Lamech had three sons, Jabal, Jubal, and Tubalcain (Genesis iv 19-22). Perhaps the dramatist thought there were only two, confusing Jubal and Tubalcain, for after the following speech, Noah is mocked by Tubal and Jabel only. They are proof of the evil behaviour for which God is destroying the world (not represented in any other version except the *VT*, see Woolf, p. 132). Mockers of Noah are mentioned in *Cursor Mundi*, 1735-40, but are neither named nor numbered. There seems to be no extant analogue to this episode, though it resembles that (popular in iconography) in which Job's 'friends' try to distract him by playing a discordant tune (see L. Reau, *Iconographie de l'Art Chrétien* (Paris, 1955-9) II, i, pp. 317-8) - Jubal was connected with musical instruments (Genesis iv 21).

2297-99. In Eastern versions, Noah's wife and one of his sons ask this question (see Woolf, pp. 133-4), so it is not necessarily a clue to the location of the production. Indeed Cornwall has such a large proportion of sea-coast that this is almost certainly a joke.

2300. Cf. The English proverb 'Words are but wind'; Tilley W833 (*whath* = 'puff').

2305. Cf. 2296.

2330 ff. Jabel's tone here resembles that of a mother placating a naughty child.

2336-8. Cf. 2147-9.

2344. *der vanar da* Cf. 2334.

2352 ff. Tubal is no doubt thinking of himself and his friends.

2355. *polatys* See Intro., p. xxi.

2378. *voydya* See note on 2171.

2379. Cf. 1303.

2399. *droge eball* lit. 'bad colt'.

2413. *quick* This may mean 'living' (*OED* a A 1), as at 2113.

2414. *chattell* See note on 405.

2419 sd. How was this done?

2435. *thaga hydnda* llt. 'their kind'.

2438. This is the only mention of Noah's three daughters-in-law, who are given speeches of their own in *Chester* and *VT*.

2441 ff. This scene seems a gesture towards the brawl between Noah and his wife which is so important in *Towneley* and *Chester*. The depiction of Mrs Noah as a shrew seems peculiar to medieval drama in England, although it is widespread in European art and folk-lore. See Cawley, p. 96; A.J.Mill, 'Noah's Wife Again', *PMLA*, XLI (1926), pp. 613-26; Woolf, pp. 138 - 44.

2443. Perhaps Mrs Noah holds up some 'treasure' here. It would be interesting to know what things she considered so valuable: perhaps her spinning materials (which symbolise fallen woman) - in *Towneley* she refuses to enter the ship until her spinning is done. In *Chester* she at first refuses to enter the Ark without her 'gossips'. 'These excuses are on a par with those in the parable made by the guests invited to the wedding feast' (Woolf, p. 140) i.e. they show the reluctance of the sinner to give up the blandishments of the world.

2457-60 Cf. *OM* 1089-92.

2467. Although the rain itself only lasted 40 days and nights, Noah and his family remained in the Ark over a year. The 'waters of the flood were on the earth' (Genesis vii, 10) and they entered the Ark on the first day of Noah's 600th year; the rain began on the 17th day of the 2nd month (Genesis vii 11); the Ark landed on Ararat on the 17th day of the seventh month of that year (Genesis viii 4); the tops of the mountains were visible on the first day of the tenth month (Genesis vii 5), after a further 40 days, Noah opened the window (Genesis viii 6), but they did not leave the Ark until the 27th day of the second month of Noah's 601st year (Genesis viii 13-14). See Allen, p. 70.

2475-8. Cf. *OM* 1157-60.

2485-6. Cf. *OM* 1173-4, where the words are spoken by Cam (= Ham).

2489. Presumably the animals sacrificed had mated while in the Ark: their species would otherwise have become extinct.

2503. The purpose of the rainbow is to remind God himself of the covenant (see Genesis ix 16), hence my emendation.

2511-2. Cf. *OM* 1211-12.

2513-5. Men were vegetarians before the Flood, see note on 1468 ff.

2513. *ehan* See note on 409.

2532 ff. Noah now speaks as epilogue. Possibly he takes off part of his costume, as he speaks of himself in the third person at 2541. Cf. *OM* 2825 ff., where the epilogue is spoken by King Solomon (Nicodemus in *PC*, Emperor in *RD*).

2542. Cf. *OM* 2843.

2547-9. Cf. *RD* 2645-6, though all the Cornish plays end with a request for music from minstrels. See J.R. Moore, 'Miracle Plays, minstrels and jigs' *PMLA* XLVIII (1933), pp. 934-5.

APPENDIX I

Extract from Richard Carew, *Survey of Cornwall* (London, 1602).

Pastimes to delight the mind, the *Cornish* men have Guary miracles, and three mens songs: and for exercise of the body, Hunting, Hawking, Shooting, Wrastling, Hurling, and such other games.

The Guary miracle, in English, a miracle-play, is a kinde of Enterlude, compiled in *Cornish* out of some scripture history, with that grossenes, which accompanied the Romanes *vetus Comedia*. For representing it, they raise an earthen Amphitheatre, in some open field, hauing the Diameter of his enclosed playne some 40. or 50. foot. The Country people flock from all sides, many miles off, to heare & see it; for they haue therein, deuils and deuices, to delight as well the eye as the eare: the players conne not their parts without booke, but are prompted by one called the Ordinary, who followeth at their back with the booke in his hand, and telleth them softly what they must pronounce aloud. Which maner once gaue occasion to a pleasant conceyted gentleman, of practising a mery pranke; for he undertaking (perhaps of set purpose) an Actor's roome, was accordingly lessoned (before-hand) by the Ordinary, that he must say after him. His turne came: quoth the Ordinarie, Goe forth man and shew thy selfe. The gentleman steps out vpon the stage, and like a bad Clarke in scripture matters, cleauing more to the letter than the sense, pronounced those words aloud. Oh (sayes the fellowe softly in his eare) you marre all the play. And with this his passion, the Actor makes the audience in like sort acquainted. Hereon the promptor falls to flat rayling & cursing in the bitterest termes he could deuise: which the Gentleman with a set gesture and countenance still soberly related, untill the Ordinary driuen at last into a madde rage, was faine to giue over all. Which trousse though it brake off the Enterlude, yet defrauded not the beholders, but dismissed them with a great deale more sport and laughter, than 20. such Guaries could have affoorded.

(pp. 71-2)

APPENDIX II

Parallel lines in *Origo Mundi*

These are God's lines unless otherwise stated.

≃ is used when there are slight variations in words; otherwise the lines are identical apart from spelling changes.

Origo Mundi	*Creacion*
lemmen pan yv nef thy'n gwrys	9 ≃ 69
an re-ma yv oberys	15 ≃ 104

Del ony onen ha try
  tas ha map yn trynyte
ny a'd wra ty then a bry
  haval d'agan face whare
ny a whyth in thy vody
  sperys may hylly bewe
ha'n bewnans pan y'n kylly
  the'n dor ty a dreyl arte
 	
Adam saf yn ban yn clor
  ha treyl the gyk ha the woys
preder my the'th whul a dor
  haval they'm a'n pen the'n troys
myns vs yn tyr hag yn mor
  warnethe kemer galloys
yn bys-ma rak dry ascor
  ty a vew bys may fy loys
	57-72 = 344-359

War bup frut losow ha has	77 = 370
Scon a onan a'th asow My a wra thy'so parow pup vr ol rag the weres	99-101= 390-2

Adam otte an puskes
ythyn a'n nef ha'n bestes
  kefrys yn tyr hag yn mor
ro thethe aga hynwyn
y a thue the'th worhemmyn
  saw na byhgh y war nep cor
	117-122= 398-403

yt'hanwaf bugh ha tarow	123 = 404(Adam)
y rof hynwyn the'n puskes	135 = 410(Adam)

Origo Mundi	*Creacion*

Rag bones ol tek ha da
  in whed dyth myns yw formyys
Aga sona ny a wra
  May fe seythves dyth hynwys
hen yw dyth a bowesva
  the pup den a vo sylwys
yn dysquythyens a henna
  ny a bowes desempys
	141 - 8 = 413-20

Eua prag na thuete nes rag cous orthyf ha talkye vn dra a won a'n gothfes	149-51 = 544-6 (Serpent)
neb a glewsys ov cane	224 = 771(Adam)
my a wra ol del vynny drov e thy'mmo dysempys ha me a ra y dybry	246-8 = 842-4

ogh trv trv my re behas
  ha re dorras an dyfen
a debel venyn hep ras
  ty ru'um tullas sur hep ken
agan corfow noth gallas
	249-53 = 851-5(Adam)

y won the wyr dev an tas	255 = 859(Adam)

Adam adam pandra wreth
  prag na theth thu'um wolcumme
drefen ov bos noeth hep queth
  ragos yth yth the gvthe
pyw a thysquethes thy'so
  the vos noeth corf tros ha bregh
lemyn an frut grath na'th fo
  mones th'y dybry hep pegh
thy'mmo vy why a ros gvrek
  honna yw ol the vlamye
a dorras an avel tek
  hag a'n dug thy'm the dastye
Aban golste worty hy
  ha gruthyl dres ov defen
	257-70 = 866-9;
	871-4;
	876-881;
	(868-9,
	876-9 Adam)

y'th whys lavur the thybry ty a wra bys y'th worfen	273-4 = 882-3
Eua prag y whruste sy tulle the bryes hep ken	277-8 = 884-5

Origo Mundi	*Creacion*
Rag ty the gola worty ha tolle the bryes len nefre gustyth th'y gorty me a orden bos benen may mohghaho hy huth hy dre wul ow gorhemmyn trogh na heb mur lavur defry benytha ny's tevyth flogh	293-300 = 891-4; 896-9
My a leuer thy's an cas rag bos thethe ioy mar vras ha my pup vr ow lesky	305-7 = 902-4(Serpent)
A das dev y'th wolowys grannt the'th whythres my a'd peys nep peyth a oel a vercy Adam yn dyweth a'n beys my a wronnt oel mercy they's ha the eua the wreghty	325-30= 935; 937-41 (935-8 Adam)
Adam ke yn mes a'n wlas troha ken pow the vewe ty the honyn the balas the wrek genes the nethe	343-6 = 972-5(Cherub)
fystynyugh troh an danas rag vmma ny wreugh tryge	349-50= 979-80(Cherub)
gorre the'n meneth tabor	429 ≃ 1070 (God in *OM*, Adam in *Creacion*)
Caym lauar ple ma abel	571 = 1142
Otte voys mernans abel the vroder prest ov kelwel a'n dor warnaf pup teller mylleges nefre re by hag ol an tyr a bywfy yv mylleges y'th ober	577-83= 1153-1159
ov molleth a rof thy'so	585 = 1161
the lef arluth a glewaf saw the face my ny welaf sur er ov gevw	587-9 = 1164-6(Cain)
lemyn dyfreth of ha gvak pur wyr dres ol tus a'n beys my ny won leuerel prak gans pup na vethaf lethys	593-6 = 1171-4(Cain)

Origo Mundi		*Creacion*
Caym ny vethyth yn della rag the lathe den mar qura ef a'n gevyth seyth kemmys	597-9	= 1176-8
Anotho mar thes preder worth y wythyes govynne	608-9	= 1191-2(Cain)
ty re'n lathes ru'm lowte	611	= 1199(Adam)
rys yw porrys lafurrye	683	= 1077 (Adam in *OM*, Cain in *Creacion*)
guyn bys vones thy'm fethys lafur ha duwon a'n bys fest pel my re'n seruyas ef	850-2	= 2005-7(Adam)

Drog yv genef gruthyl den
precins haual thy'm certen
rag cole orth vn venen
  gulan ef re gollas an plas
a'm luf thyghyow a wrussen
pan wruge dres ov defen
mes a parathys lowen
  an el whare a'n goras
 	
ow spyrys ny drye nefre
  yn corf map den vyth yn beys
ha reson yv ha prage
  rag y vos kyc methel gurys
nynsus den ort ov seruye
  len ha guyryon me a greys
yn ol an beys sav noe
  ha'y wrek ha'y flehes kefrys
	917-32	= 2212-23;
		2225-28

Noe mar luen yv an beys
  lemyn a scherewynsy
may thew theweth dynythys
  ynno a gyk pup huny
gans pegh mar vr ev flerys
  na allaf sparie na moy
hep gul dyel a ver speys
  war pep ol sur marnas ty
 	
Rag henna fystyn ke gura
  gorhel a blankos playnyys
hag ynno lues trygva
  romes y a vyth gylwys
aves hag agy yn-ta
  gans pek bethens stanchvrys
ha tryhans keuelyn da
  an lester a vyth a hys
	941-64	= 2245-52;
		2255-70

... Cont'd ...

Origo Mundi	*Creacion*

... cont'd ...
ha hanter cans keuelyn
  yn-weth ty a wra y les
yn vhelder my a vyn
  dek-warn-ugans y vos gures
war tu dylarg daras yn
  ty a wra yv port hynwes
tresters dretho ty a pyn
  a-drus rag na vo degees	

A bub eghen a kunda
  gorow ha benow yn weth
aga gora ty a wra
  yn the worhel aberveth
pup maner bos yn bys-ma
  vs the dybry may telet
rag den ha best magata
  yn the lester ty a fet
	989-996 = 2271-78

Arluth cuf the arghadow	= 2279(Noah)

Marow yv pup tra ese
  spyrys a vewnans ynno
my a worhemmyn whare
  the'n glaw na moy na wrello
	1089-92 = 2457-60

Noe my a worhemmyn thy's
  ke yn mes a'th worhel scon
the wrek ha'th flehas kefrys
  ethyn bestes ha prevyon
	1157-60 = 2475-78

yn dewellens pecadow gul alter sur da vye	1173-4= 2485-6(Cam(=Ham) in *OM*, Noah in *Creacion*)
cresseugh collenweugh kefrys an nor veys a dus arte	1211-12 = 2511-12
a-vorow devg a dermyn	2843 ≃ 2542 (Epilogue in *OM*, Noah in *Creacion*)

APPENDIX III

The generations of Adam

The following table is based on the information given in Genesis iv-vi. Those who appear in the *Creacion* are capitalised. (No women's names are given in these chapters of Genesis other than those of Lamech's wives).

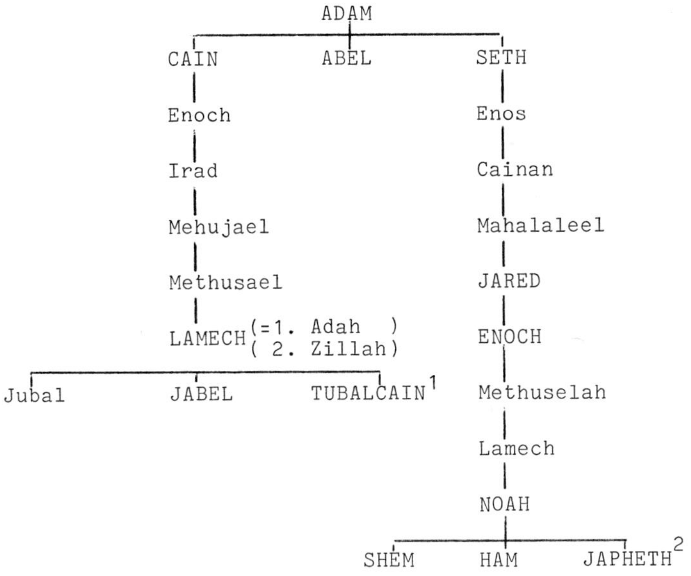

1. See note on 2295 sp.
2. See note on 2287 ff.

APPENDIX IV

Table for conversion to Stokes' line-numbering

There are slight differences between the line-numbering of this edition and that of Stokes, partly because some numbers are misprinted in his edition[1] and partly because twice I print two half-lines where he has one continuous line.[2] There is never more than a two line difference but since all philological work up till now has relied on Stokes' edition (and there is now a Cornish computer) I append this conversion table.

Stokes	*this edition*
1-63	1-63
65-152	64-151
153	152-153
154-199	154-199
200	200-201
201-773	202-774
775-838	775-838
840-1006	839-1005
1007	omitted (see collation at 1005)
1008-1614	1006-1612
[1614]-1774	1613-1773
[1774]-1939	1774-1939
[1939]-2548	1940-2549

1. There are only four lines between Stokes' 60-65, 770-775, 835-840; and there are six lines between his 1610-1615, 1770-1775, 1935-1940.

2. *Creacion* 152-153, 200-201. (There are virgules in *MS* dividing these lines).